T0334573

Cambridge Elements ≡

Elements in the Problems of God
edited by
Michael L. Peterson
Asbury Theological Seminary

C.S. LEWIS AND THE PROBLEM OF GOD

David A. Werther
University of Wisconsin – Madison

CAMBRIDGE
UNIVERSITY PRESS

CAMBRIDGE
UNIVERSITY PRESS

Shaftesbury Road, Cambridge CB2 8EA, United Kingdom

One Liberty Plaza, 20th Floor, New York, NY 10006, USA

477 Williamstown Road, Port Melbourne, VIC 3207, Australia

314–321, 3rd Floor, Plot 3, Splendor Forum, Jasola District Centre,
New Delhi – 110025, India

103 Penang Road, #05–06/07, Visioncrest Commercial, Singapore 238467

Cambridge University Press is part of Cambridge University Press & Assessment,
a department of the University of Cambridge.

We share the University's mission to contribute to society through the pursuit of
education, learning and research at the highest international levels of excellence.

www.cambridge.org
Information on this title: www.cambridge.org/9781009500395

DOI: 10.1017/9781009283212

First published 2024

A catalogue record for this publication is available from the British Library.

ISBN 978-1-009-50039-5 Hardback
ISBN 978-1-009-28324-3 Paperback
ISSN 2754-8724 (online)
ISSN 2754-8716 (print)

C.S. Lewis and the Problem of God

Elements in the Problems of God

DOI: 10.1017/9781009283212
First published online: April 2024

David A. Werther
University of Wisconsin – Madison

Author for correspondence: David A. Werther, dwerther@gmail.com

Abstract: Understanding C.S. Lewis's vocation is essential for reading his works well, as is knowing how he came to it: his long and winding philosophical journey and recurring experiences of "Joy." Lewis discounted "proofs" in philosophical theology but offered key arguments in support of theism per se, and Christianity in particular. His account of "mere Christianity" shows the centrality of self-determination, an emphasis on Christ's human nature, and a relativizing of atonement theories. Finally, Lewis's understanding of faith, his attempts to make sense of petitionary and imprecatory prayers, and his emphasis on theosis/deification, are considered.

This Element also has a video abstract: www.cambridge.org/EPOG_Werther

Keywords: God, C.S. Lewis, Mere Christianity, theistic arguments

ISBNs: 9781009500395 (HB), 9781009283243 (PB), 9781009283212 (OC)
ISSNs: 2754-8724 (online), 2754-8716 (print)

Contents

1 Approaching C.S. Lewis

1.1 Vocation

C.S. Lewis's tutor, William T. Kirkpatrick, fondly known as "The Great Knock," wrote to Albert Lewis about his son's prospects: "You may make a writer or a scholar of him, but you'll not make anything else. You may make up your mind to *that*" (Lewis 1955b: 183). Kirkpatrick was right on both counts: Lewis became both a writer and a scholar. His initial ambition was to be a poet, and his first publications were a collection of poems, *Spirits in Bondage*, first published in 1919 (Lewis 2015: 73–123), and a lyrical poem, *Dymer*, published in 1926 (2015: 145–218). Lewis would write poetry for the rest of his life, although his ambition to be a great poet would fade.

Lewis's scholarship reflected his studies at Oxford, initially in Classical Languages and Literature, together with Philosophy and Ancient History, and to increase his job prospects, English Literature. Lewis's work in philosophy is apparent in *The Abolition of Man*, *Miracles*, and essays like "The Humanitarian Theory of Punishment." His literary scholarship is evidenced in works such as *The Allegory of Love*, *English Literature in the 16th Century Excluding Drama*, *Studies in Words*, and *The Discarded Image*.

Lewis's fiction includes his children's stories (The Chronicles of Narnia, in seven books), a science fiction trilogy (*Out of the Silent Planet*, *Perelandra*, and *That Hideous Strength*), a reinterpretation of the myth of Cupid and Psyche (*Till We Have Faces*), as well as satire (*Screwtape Letters*, and *The Great Divorce*).

Among Lewis's apologetic writings is *The Problem of Pain*, the work that caught the attention of J.W. Welch (Hooper 1996: 303), Director of the BBC's Religious Broadcasting Department, and led to an invitation to do a series of radio broadcasts that would become his best-known apologetic work, and one of the most influential Christian books in the twentieth century, *Mere Christianity*. A survey of church leaders conducted in 2000 by the influential American evangelical magazine *Christianity Today* ranked it first among the "100 books that had a significant effect on Christians in this century" (Marsden 2016:1).

Lewis wrote four autobiographical volumes: *All My Road Before Me: The Diary of C. S. Lewis, 1922–1927*; *The Pilgrim's Regress*, a semi-autobiographical allegorical account of his conversion; *Surprised by Joy*, a more accessible and mature conversion account; and *A Grief Observed*, Lewis's heart-wrenching reflections after the death of his wife Joy.

Kirkpatrick's assessment of Lewis's prospects as a scholar and writer was spot-on. He would have been shocked, though, to learn that the young man he tutored, who thrived on reading and reflection, would spend so much time outside of his study: lecturing to the RAF (Babbage 1980; Gilmore 2005); addressing the nation on the BBC (Phillips 2002); enjoying the companionship of a circle of Christian friends, the Inklings (Duriez 2015b; Glyer 2007; Zaleski and Zaleski 2015); and serving as the president of the Oxford Socratic Club (Aldwinkle 2015; Hooper 1979; Lewis 1970: 126–8; Mitchell 1997). Of his time studying with Kirkpatrick, Lewis wrote, "For if I could please myself I would always live as I lived there" (1955b: 141), and emphasized a key component of those pleasant days: "it is an essential of the happy life that a man would have almost no mail and never dread the postman's knock" (143). At this time, Lewis loathed interruptions and interference. After his conversion, he had a different perspective on such things as "the postman's knock":

> The great thing, if one can, is to stop regarding all the unpleasant things as interruptions of one's "own," or "real" life. The truth is of course that what one calls the interruptions are precisely one's real life – the life God is sending one day by day. (Lewis 2004b: 595)

From Lewis's public persona and his belief that he had "a duty to answer fully" letters from "serious inquirers" (504), "grew hundreds – eventually thousands – of letters replete with spiritual guidance to a wide range of inquirers among them spiritual seekers, recent converts . . . others struggling with temptation and guilt, and many healthy Christians simply in search of sound teaching" (Dorsett 2004: 116).

Although Lewis's writings and activities were diverse, they all reflected a sense of vocation. At the outbreak of World War II, Lewis gave a sermon "Learning in War-Time," in which he addressed the topic of vocation and underscored two principles:

All we do should be done to the glory of God:

> All our merely natural activities will be accepted, if they are offered to God, even the humblest, and all of them, even the noblest, will be sinful if they are not. (1980: 25)

> The work of a Beethoven and the work of a charwoman become spiritual on precisely the same condition, that of being offered to God, of being done humbly "as to the Lord." (26)

A person's interests are a good indication of his vocation:

> An appetite for these things [knowledge and beauty] exists in the human mind, and God makes no appetite in vain. We can therefore pursue knowledge as such, and beauty as such, in the sure confidence that by doing so we are either advancing to the vision of God ourselves or indirectly helping others to do so. (27)

For Lewis himself, a vocation-shaping circumstance came in the form of a physical defect:

> What drove me to write was the extreme manual clumsiness from which I have always suffered. I attribute it to a physical defect which my brother and I both inherit from our father; we have only one joint in the thumb. The upper joint (that furthest from the nail) is visible, but it is a mere sham; we cannot bend it. But whatever the cause, nature laid on me from birth an utter incapacity to make anything. With pencil and pen I was handy enough ... but with a tool or a bat ... I have always been unteachable. It was this that forced me to write. (Lewis 1955b: 12)

While Lewis's physical defect contributed to his sense of vocation, it was not what he would call a life-bending circumstance:

> Our life has bends as well as extension: moments at which we realize that we have just turned some great corner, and that everything, for better or worse, will always henceforth be different. (Lewis 1961: 36)

The great turning point in Lewis's life was his realization that Jesus Christ is the Son of God. That change led to a special calling: "Since my conversion, it has seemed my particular task to tell the outside world what all Christians believe" (quoted in Hooper 1996: 297).

For Further Reading: In *C.S. Lewis's List* (Werther & Werther 2015), ten Lewis scholars introduce and discuss the works Lewis identified as having had the greatest impact on his sense of vocation. Will Vaus devotes a trilogy to these works (2014; 2015; 2018). For a selection of Lewis's letters of spiritual counsel, see (Lewis 2008).

1.2 *Mere Christianity*

That calling was nowhere more apparent than in *Mere Christianity*, where he sought "to explain and defend the belief that has been common to nearly all Christians at all times" (Lewis 2001b: viii), and – by extension – in The Chronicles of Narnia:

> At some point during the time he was writing the Chronicles (between 1949 and 1953) Lewis revised the three separate BBC talks into a single volume ... Thus *Mere Christianity* was fresh in Lewis's mind during the time he was writing the Chronicles and that may account, in part at least, for the numerous parallels in imagery and word choice between it and various Chronicles. Those parallels, in several instances, seem to be central to the plot or structure of the stories and to have a significance far beyond clarification of a particular idea or doctrine in the stories. (Schakel 1980: xiii)

In *The Fame of C.S. Lewis*, Stephanie L. Derrick underscores the ongoing influence of The Chronicles of Narnia and *Mere Christianity:*

> While there are no official sales numbers available, one of Lewis's heirs recently claimed that over 100 million copies of the Narnia books had been sold in more than forty languages ... His non-fiction book *Mere Christianity* is annually one of the top fifty bestselling religious titles, at 250,000 copies a year and another 50,000 in audio books. (Derrick 2018: 2)

In contrast to these bestsellers, Lewis's *An Experiment in Criticism* is one of the literary writings Mark Neal and Jerry Root include in their volume, *The Neglected Lewis*. In *An Experiment in Criticism*, Lewis makes a fundamental distinction between receiving and using a work:

> A work of (whatever) art can be either "received" or "used." When we "receive" it we exert our senses and imagination and various other powers according to the pattern invented by the artist. When we use it we treat it as assistance for our own activities. (1960a: 88)

> The first demand any work of art makes upon us is surrender. Look. Listen. Receive. Get yourself out of the way. (There is no good asking first whether the work before you deserves such a surrender, for until you have surrendered you cannot possibly find out.) (19)

Although Lewis had art and literature in mind, the receiving/using distinction can be applied more broadly to cover not only The Chronicles of Narnia, but *Mere Christianity* as well. In order to understand what sort of work *Mere Christianity* is, it is helpful to know how it came about. The first step in receiving a work is to identify its genre. *Mere Christianity* combines three earlier works, each consisting of scripts from Lewis's BBC broadcasts, with minimal editing (Marsden 2016: 189–91). Lewis was allotted ten or fifteen minutes for each talk. The BBC's 1942 handbook gives a good indication of the kind of talk the BBC wanted:

> In a time of uncertainty and questioning it is the responsibility of the Church – and of religious broadcasting as one of its most powerful voices – to declare the truth about God and His relation to men. It has to expound the Christian faith in terms that can be easily understood by ordinary men and women, and to examine the ways in which that faith can be applied to present-day society during these difficult times. (quoted in Phillips 2002: 78)

Within these parameters, Lewis's goal was to "to explain and defend the belief that has been common to nearly all Christians at all times" (Lewis 2001b: viii). Continually focusing on Lewis's objective is the key to "receiving" *Mere Christianity*.

Lewis reported that there was something of a consensus regarding his identification of core Christian claims: "So far as I can judge from reviews and letters written to me, the book did at least succeed in presenting an agreed upon or common, or central, or 'mere' Christianity" (2001b: xi). Given Lewis's coverage of the objectivity of the moral law, the deity of Christ, and the doctrine of the Trinity, "the central Christian message" (the atonement), the cardinal and theological virtues, and so forth, the consensus is not surprising.

Identifying core doctrines is one matter; staying within that core is another. Consider the doctrine of purgatory. Lewis scholar Jerry Walls writes, "Lewis's belief in purgatory flows easily and consistently out of his theology, particularly his [transformational] account of the nature of salvation" (Walls 2012: 157). The theology Walls has in mind finds expression in *Mere Christianity* (2001b: 158–63). Though Lewis does not draw undue attention to that implication of transformational salvation in *Mere Christianity* – the word "purgatory" nowhere appears in *Mere Christianity*, as it does in *Letters to Malcolm Chiefly on Prayer* (108–9) – the implication is there: "Whatever suffering it may cost you in your early life, whatever inconceivable purification it may cost you after death" (2001b: 202), Christ will not rest "until you are literally perfect" (202). If Walls is right, and an affirmation of purgatory is not among central Christian beliefs, then Lewis seems to have strayed from core Christian beliefs. What might Lewis have said in response? He might well have agreed, and – as already noted – pointed out that he avoided using the word "purgatory" because he did not want to highlight a divisive doctrine. However, he might have argued that because salvation is transformational, he could not have both correctly portrayed salvation and completely avoided the implication of purgatory.

Identifying basic beliefs is but one step. After that comes explanation and defense, and both admit of degrees. It would be inappropriate to hold Lewis to the same standard as a theologian writing for scholars. When Lewis thought he was being judged according to that standard, he wrote:

> My task was therefore simply that of a *translator* – one turning Christian doctrine, or what he believed to be such, into the vernacular, into language that unscholarly people would attend to and could understand. For this purpose a style more guarded, more *nuancé*, finelier shaded ... would have been worse than useless. (Lewis 1970: 183)

> Suppose the image [comparing the Trinity, three persons while remaining one being, to a cube, six squares while remaining one cube] is vulgar. If it gets across to the unbeliever what the unbeliever desperately needs to know, the vulgarity must be endured. (182)

Readers who do not hold *Mere Christianity* to an inappropriately high academic standard may nonetheless point out shortcomings in some of Lewis's explanations and defenses. If they do, they may find themselves in the company of the author himself. For example, when Lewis wrote on the Christian doctrine of marriage, he acknowledged that his perspective was limited: "I have never been married myself, and therefore can only speak second hand" (2001b: 104). "If you disagree with me, of course, you will say, 'He knows nothing about it, he is not married.' You may quite possibly be right." (2001b: 109). And regarding his defense of the deity of Christ, he came to recognize the need for a more comprehensive account: "something must be said about the historicity" (Lewis 1970: 101).

Receiving Lewis's work well – reading it in light of his stated goal – requires careful thought. The result may be agnosticism, acceptance of Christianity, or even rejection of it. Lewis was clear: "I am not asking anyone to accept Christianity if his best reasoning tells him that the weight of evidence is against it" (Lewis 2001b: 140).

For Further Reading: Thomas C. Oden devotes three volumes (2001a; 2001b; 2001c) to expressing "an ordered view of the faith of the Christian community upon which there has been generally substantial agreement between the traditions of East and West, including Catholic, Protestant, and Orthodox" (2001a: ix).

1.3 The Chronicles of Narnia

As with *Mere Christianity*, so too with The Chronicles of Narnia: When determining the nature of this work it is helpful to know how it came about. In his essay, "It All Began with a Picture," Lewis wrote:

> One thing I am sure of. All my seven Narnian books, and my three science-fiction books, began with seeing pictures in my head. At first they were not a story, just pictures. The *Lion* all began with a picture of a Faun carrying an umbrella and parcels in a snowy wood. This picture had been in my mind since I was about sixteen. (1982: 53)

Lewis explained in an essay, "On Three Ways of Writing for Children," how a story may emerge from pictures:

> I have never exactly "made" a story. With me the process is much more like bird-watching than like either talking or building. I see pictures. Some of these pictures have a common flavour, almost a common smell, which groups them together. Keep quiet and watch and they will begin joining themselves up. If you were very lucky ... a whole set might join themselves so consistently that there you had a complete story; without doing anything yourself.

But more often (in my experience always) there are gaps. Then at last you have to do some deliberate inventing, have to contrive reasons why these characters should be in these various places doing these various things. (1982: 41)

As Lewis wrote in "Sometimes Fairy Stories May Say Best What's to Be Said," his deliberate inventing was not a matter of fitting in predetermined morals:

Some people think that I began by asking myself how I could say something about Christianity to children; then fixed on the fairy tale as an instrument . . . then drew up a list of basic Christian truths and hammered out "allegories" to embody them. This is all pure moonshine. I couldn't write in that way at all. (Lewis 1982: 46)

Rather, any moral from the author should arise "inevitably from the whole cast of the author's mind" (42), "from whatever spiritual roots you have succeeded in striking during the whole course of your life" (41). What arises from pictures in the author's mind and spiritual roots will find its way into print only if the author can find an appropriate form for his material:

In the Author's mind there bubbles up every now and then the material for a story. . . . This ferment leads to nothing unless it is accompanied with the longing for a Form: verse or prose, short story, novel, play or what not. (45)

In the case of The Chronicles of Narnia:

As these images sorted themselves into events (i.e., became a story) they seemed to demand no love interest and no close psychology. But the Form which excludes these things is the fairy tale. And the moment I thought of that I fell in love with the Form itself. (46)

In *Reading with the Heart: The Way into Narnia*, Peter J. Schakel aptly describes the Narnian stories as fairy tales embodying fantasy and romance:

As fairy tales, then, the Chronicles will be characterized by strangeness and wonder, usually produced by magic, but at the same time, as fantasies, they must be believable and have an internal consistency. Such believability is attained, in fairy tales which are also fantasies, by creation of a separate, "enchanted" world into which characters and readers are taken. (Schakel 1980: 2)

In the case of the Chronicles of Narnia, one must begin with the understanding that, within their form as fairy tales, they employ the narrative pattern, or *mythos*, of romance. The romance is characterized by a standard plot, one of quest or adventure . . . it is set in a courtly or chivalric age, often of highly developed manners and chivalry; it stresses knightly ideals of courage, honor, mercifulness to an opponent. (11)

And, just as importantly, C.S. Lewis himself underscored that The Chronicles are not allegories:

> You are mistaken when you think that everything in the book "represents" something in this world. Things do that in *The Pilgrim's Progress* but I'm not writing in that way. I did not say to myself "Let us represent Jesus as He really is in our world by a Lion in Narnia": I said "Let us *suppose* that there were a land like Narnia and that the Son of God, as He became a Man in our world, became a Lion there, and then imagine what would happen." If you think about it, you will see that it is quite a different thing. (2007: 479–80)

In sum, The Chronicles of Narnia are suppositions in the form of fairy tales embodying fantasy and romance.

Having identified the sort of work The Chronicles of Narnia is, we see that to "receive" them, we must keep in mind that Lewis has given us a suppositional world to live within, not an extended allegory. The perspective Peter J. Schakel advances in *Reading with the Heart* seems to be the right one to take:

> The key to the approach of this book, then, is that it assumes the Chronicles are not dependent on works or ideas outside of themselves, either through allegory or allusion. They depict secondary worlds, separate and self-contained, and they are to be "received" as such, through the imagination and the emotions. (Schakel 1980: xiv)

> At times readers who know the Bible well will find phrases or situations in the Chronicles which remind them of biblical phrases or situations. Such reminders are natural and to be expected: they are part of the ripple effect within the whole of literature. But the recognition of the allusions should be almost automatic, a tidbit which enriches the experience of the reader ... The effect is spoiled if the allusion must be pointed out and explained. (1980: xiii)

Readers who know theology well need to keep in mind that some of the "allusions" they see may be "illusory." For instance, Trevor Anderson (295–96) calls into question Douglas Wilson's assertion that "The nature of the lion's [Aslan's] death ... is seen as a very definite [limited] atonement" (Wilson 2014: 73).

In the same way, we must bear in mind Lewis's "*mythos,* of romance." Here again, Schakel is helpful:

> Each *mythos* has over the centuries developed a set of conventions, the "rules" by which the "game" of that type is played. Like the rules of a game, the conventions of a genre must be accepted if one is to enjoy the story as written. . . . Recognizing conventions, particularly conventions from the romance tradition, can help prevent misunderstanding of the Chronicles. The Chronicles have been criticized, for example, for being racist, sexist and overly violent. To criticize Lewis fairly, one must consider the conventions of the *mythos* within which he is writing. (1980: 13)

Schakel goes on to show how Lewis not only works within the conventions of romance but also departs from them. So, for example, while Lewis did not dispense with violence altogether, he downplayed it relative to expectations of the genre.

Some may find even Lewis's tempered romantic conventions too much to take. They may object to The Chronicles – not because they fail to present us with a consistent and coherent suppositional world – but because they find the suppositional world suspect on moral grounds. Richard Purtill correctly points out that an objection along the lines of "These ideas are false and you do a disservice by propagating them" is philosophical in nature and as such "must be backed by argument" (Purtill 2006: 38). Without appropriate argumentation such objections run the risk of "chronology snobbery": the "uncritical acceptance of the intellectual climate common to our own age and the assumption that whatever has gone out of date is on that account discredited" (Lewis 1955b: 207). To avoid this error one must find out "Was it ever refuted (and if so by whom, where, and how conclusively) or did it merely die away as fashions do?" (207–8).

For Further Reading: Leland Ryken and Marjorie Lamp Mead provide a valuable resource for looking at *The Lion, the Witch, and the Wardrobe* "through lenses gathered from Lewis's literary criticism on the subject of literature and literary analysis" (2005: 10). See also Devin Brown's essay, "Are the Chronicles of Narnia Sexist?" (2015).

1.4 On the Reading of Old Books

In "On the Reading of Old Books," Lewis encouraged the reading of older works as a way to combat our cultural myopia. Eighty years ago, he wrote:

> Every age has its own outlook. It is specially good at seeing certain truths and specially liable to make certain mistakes. We all, therefore, need the books that will correct the characteristic mistakes of our period. And that means the old books. . . . The only palliative is to keep the clean sea breeze of the centuries blowing through our minds, and this can be done only by reading the old books. (Lewis 1970: 202)

More than 100 years have passed since Lewis's first work *Spirits in Bondage* appeared, and 60 years since his last, *Letters to Malcolm Chiefly on Prayer* – enough time that Lewis's own works fall under the category of older writings, especially since Lewis claimed that his works reflected still older periods. So then, approaching Lewis's works we should expect some disharmony with our own cultural climate. And sometimes the disharmony may be jarring. But that is no reason to shy away from Lewis's work or any other older works. Indeed, looking at the world through a different set of eyes is one of the reasons for turning to older works in the first place.

And if we turn to Lewis's work to feel "the clear sea breeze of the centuries," we would do well to acquaint ourselves with the breadth of Lewis's work. A good rule of thumb would be that after reading a book in one genre of Lewis's writings, e.g. apologetics, not to allow yourself another until you have read a work in a different genre, e.g. philosophy, fiction, literary criticism, theology or autobiography.

For Further Reading: In the *Neglected Lewis*, Mark Neal and Jerry Root examine eight of Lewis's literary works to provide "a starting point to whet the interest of those who love C.S. Lewis but are not familiar with these works" (2020: 10). Joel D. Heck lists all of Lewis's works, numbering over 500, in chronological order: www.joelheck.com/resources/TheCompleteWorksofCSLewis.pdf. See also Walter Hooper's excellent bibliography (2005a). For a look at Lewis's own reading, Joel D. Heck draws upon Lewis's diary, *All My Road Before Me*, and lists the 407 books Lewis read from April 1, 1922 through March 2, 1927 (Heck 2005, 145–56).

2 "A Road Very Rarely Trodden" *The Pilgrim's Regress*

2.1 The End of All Settled Happiness

Shortly after his sixteenth birthday, Lewis engaged in "one of the worst acts of my life" (Lewis 1955b: 161). He allowed himself "to be prepared for confirmation, and confirmed, and to make my first Communion" at St. Mark's Church in Belfast, Ireland, on December 6, 1914, and did so "in total disbelief, acting a part, eating and drinking my own condemnation," knowing "very well that I was acting a lie with the greatest possible solemnity" (161). Lewis's shameful behavior raises several questions: *Was there a time prior to this act when Lewis did believe the gospel? If so, how did he lose his faith, and why did he allow himself to go through confirmation "in total disbelief"?*

Thomas Hamilton, Lewis's maternal grandfather and vicar of St. Mark's Church, baptized Clive Staples Lewis on January 29, 1899, two months after his birth on November 29, 1898. Insofar as Lewis had any faith growing up, it was propositional, not personal: "I was taught the usual things . . . I naturally accepted what I was told but I cannot remember feeling much interest in it" (7). He became "an effective believer" during the days at his first boarding school (September 1908–July 1910), when he "heard the doctrines of Christianity (as distinct from general "uplift") taught by men who obviously believed them" (33).

Between baptism and boarding school, Lewis had his first experiences of a desire unlike any other, as well as an unparalleled loss from which he would never completely recover. Lewis used the word "Joy" to distinguish this superlative desire, "an unsatisfied desire which is itself more desirable than any satisfaction" (17–18), from pleasure and happiness. Unlike happiness, Joy might be classified as a certain sort of grief (18); unlike pleasure, Joy is never under our control (18). As with pleasure and happiness, anyone who has experienced Joy will want to experience it again and again. The significance Lewis attached to Joy may seem out of proportion to the circumstances of its occurrence: remembering a toy garden his brother had made in a biscuit tin; encountering the "Idea of Autumn" in Beatrix Potter's *Squirrel Nutkin*; reading lines found in Longfellow's "Saga of King Olaf": "I heard a voice that cried, Balder the Beautiful / Is dead, is dead" (16–17). Of Longfellow's lines, Lewis commented:

> I knew nothing about Balder; but instantly I was uplifted into huge regions of northern sky, I desired with almost sickening intensity something never to be described (except that it is cold, spacious, severe, pale, and remote) and then ... at the very same moment already falling out of that desire and wishing I were back in it. (17)

Lewis would experience Joy again, but the loss he suffered was final. Lewis was nine years old when his mother Flora died, on August 23, 1908. Flora's death was preceded by the death of Lewis's grandfather, Richard Lewis, earlier that year on the 2nd of April, and followed by the death of an uncle, Joseph Lewis, on the 3rd of September (Heck 2022b: 26). Prior to Flora's passing, Lewis prayed for her recovery and afterwards for God to bring her back to life. In retrospect, he would come to see that the essence of prayer is communion with God, an awesome Judge and Savior, and that he was treating God as a magician. At the time, Flora's death meant "all settled happiness, all that was tranquil and reliable, disappeared from my life" (Lewis 1955b: 21).

2.2 Finding and Losing Faith

Within a month of his mother's death, Lewis was packed off to Wynyard, a boarding school in Hertfordshire, England. To get a sense of Lewis's unhappiness at that school, note that in his spiritual autobiography, *Surprised by Joy*, he used the name of a Nazi concentration camp, Belsen, to refer to it (24). One might dispute the appropriateness of Lewis's concentration-camp comparison, but what is beyond dispute is that the school's headmaster caned the students and was eventually declared insane (Downing 2002: 36–37). Looking back on his life, in a letter to Bede Griffiths, Lewis referred to the death of his mother and his traumatic school experiences as among the causes contributing to his unbelief (Lewis 2004b: 747). That Lewis would, for a time, come to accept the Christian faith and "become an effective believer" (Lewis 1955b: 33) during

his days at Belsen, speaks volumes about his experiences at the church where he
heard Christian doctrine affirmed by those who truly believed it. In terms of the
distinction Lewis made in his essay "Is Theism Important?" it was at this time
that Lewis moved from "a settled intellectual assent" to "trust" (Lewis 1970:
172–74).

Following Lewis's time at Belsen (1908–1910), he returned to Belfast for
a half term at Campbell College in September 1910. Lewis again returned to
England and attended Cherbourg House in Malvern, which he referred to as
"Chartres." When Lewis came to Chartres, Joy – that "inconsolable longing"
that had meant so much to him – was conspicuously absent from his life; "not
even the memory or the desire of it remained" (Lewis 1955b: 72). That soon
changed when he saw in a literary publication the words, "Siegfried and the
Twilight of the Gods," with an illustration by Arthur Rackham (72). That
experience led to a fascination with Wagner and Norse Mythology, such that
Lewis came close to feeling about the Norse Gods what he ought to have felt for
the Christian God (thankfulness for His glory). Lewis was, however, under no
illusions that the world of Northernness was anything but imaginary (82).

Lewis's discovery of Northernness and his recovery of Joy were matched by
a loss of faith. It was at Chartres that he ceased to be a Christian. Contributing to
Lewis's unbelief were an introduction to the occult, frustrating experiences
praying, studies in classics, and the argument from Un-Design. Lewis's acquaintance with the occult came through "Miss C," the matron of the school. She was
"one of the most selfless people I have ever known" and hopelessly confused,
"floundering in the mazes of Theosophy, Rosicrucianism, Spiritualism; the whole
Anglo-American Occultist tradition" (59). Interactions with her sparked in Lewis
a passion for the occult (59–60), though the passion was never to become
a practice: "I have killed no chickens" (Lewis 2013: 20). The real harm was
lost confidence in the Christian creeds.

While Lewis's assurance in the creeds was crumbling, his prayer life was
imploding. Believing that a prayer was genuine only if the petitioner's mind did
not wander – and desperately wanting to get it right – Lewis began to obsess
over the authenticity of his prayers. As a result, praying became a painful
introspective experience (Lewis 1955b: 61–62). Studies in classics also took
their toll on Lewis's faith. Lewis noted that his teachers took it for granted that
the religious views of Virgil and other classical authors were false. Why then
make an exception for Christian beliefs? (62–63). Lewis decided not to and
reveled in his newfound freedom: "At last I could say to the universe 'Mind
your own business.' I had some department, however small, in which I was
supreme and unchallenged. And this, I am convinced, is the permanent charm of
unbelief" (Lewis 2013: 29).

Lewis's unbelief fit well with the "Argument from Undesign" (Lewis 1955b: 65). In *The Problem of Pain*, Lewis outlined the key elements of "undesign": most of the universe "consists of empty space, completely dark and unimaginably cold" (Lewis 2001d: 1); "creatures cause pain by being born, and live by inflicting pain, and in pain they mostly die" (2); our history consists mostly of "crime, war, disease, and terror" (2); in the end, "All stories will come to nothing: all life will turn out in the end to have been a transitory and senseless contortion upon the idiotic face of infinite matter" (3).

Losing one's faith is one matter; going through the motions of confirmation "in total disbelief" is another. Cowardice was the immediate cause of Lewis's hypocrisy; he wished to avoid the awful interactions he envisioned with his father were he to confess his unbelief. Cowardice, as Lewis came to see, is no small matter. Echoing Samuel Johnson, he wrote, "where courage is not, no other virtue can survive except by accident" (Lewis 1955b: 161).

2.3 Reason and Imagination

When Eric Fenn of the BBC asked Lewis if he would give an account of his return to faith, Lewis demurred, "Not my pigeon, I think. My own history was so mixed up with technical philosophy as to be useless to the general [public]" (Lewis 2004b: 568). In the preface to the third edition of *The Pilgrim's Regress*, Lewis described his philosophical long and winding road as passing from "'popular realism' to Philosophical Idealism; from Idealism to Pantheism; from Pantheism to Theism; and from Theism to Christianity" (Lewis 1958b: 5). In a letter to Mr. More, he used slightly different language, describing his journey as "from materialism to idealism, from idealism to Pantheism, from pantheism to theism, and from theism to Christianity" (Lewis 2004b: 145).

Notwithstanding the role of "technical philosophy" in Lewis's path to faith, when Lewis wrote his spiritual autobiography he prefaced his account with the caveat, "How far the story matters to anyone but myself depends upon the degree to which others have experienced what I call 'joy'" (Lewis 1955b: vii), and described his story as "suffocatingly subjective" (viii). As a courtesy to his readers he "tried so to write the first chapter that those who can't bear such a story will see at once what they are in for and close the book with the least waste of time" (viii). To be sure, philosophy is not absent from that account, but neither is it the primary focus. In "Early Prose Joy," Lewis wrote about both the role of "technical philosophy" and Joy in his return to faith, but sharply distinguished between them:

> In the first part I have described how my imaginative life [cf. "joy"] led me at
> last to the belief in a timeless <u>realissimum</u> which is not an experience but the
> heart's desire: in this part I have to tell how my intellectual life led me to

theism. It may be supposed that there is some artifice in this separation of my
experience from thinking. If there is, it is not my artifice. I divide the story
into watertight compartments because I lived the first twenty five years in
watertight compartments. I suspected no relation between the two until the
very eve of that day when the divine plot unmasked itself. (2013: 27–28)

In the following account, Lewis's return to faith proceeds chronologically,
weaving the roles of reason and Joy together. After Chartres Lewis attended
Malvern College, where he continued to explore Norse mythology, writing
a tragedy, *Loki Bound*, in which Loki cautions Odin against creation and then
opposes him when he disregards Loki's warning. Thor sides with Odin and
attempts to use force to bring Loki in line; Loki looks down upon Thor for his
might-makes-right approach. In all of this, Lewis came to see that Loki was
a projection of himself. He resented "the Bloods," Malvern's ruling elite
students, for using their status and power to make his life miserable, and wished,
like Loki, to assert his superiority.

A theme in *Loki Bound* is the desire to be left alone. Loki asked, "Why should
creatures have the burden of existence forced on them without their consent?"
(Lewis 1955b: 115). Never mind that existing is a necessary condition for
consent. Lewis's anger was getting the best of his reason: "I was at this time
living ... in a whirl of contradictions. I maintained that God did not exist. I was
also very angry with God for not existing. I was equally angry with Him for
creating a world" (115).

From Malvern College, Lewis went to Great Bookham to be tutored by
William Kirkpatrick. When he arrived, his "Atheism and Pessimism were
fully formed" (139–40); he believed "in nothing but atoms and evolution and
military service" (174). But seeing the world as a "meaningless dance of atoms"
came at a price: "Nearly all that I loved I believed to be imaginary; nearly all that
I believed to be real I thought grim and meaningless" (170). There was a payoff
though: "at least it [Kirkpatrick's rationalism] was free of the Christian God"
(171). Lewis found this being particularly odious because he was "a transcen-
dental Interferer" and "No word in my vocabulary expressed deeper hatred than
the word *Interference*" (172).

During his time at Great Bookham, Lewis began to harbor some doubts about
materialism. He greatly respected the poet Yeats and knew that Yeats believed in
Magic. Perhaps Yeats was right to reject materialism. Perhaps there was more
than a "meaningless dance of atoms," and something other than the Christian
God. With that possibility in mind, "all the old Occultist lore, and all the old
excitement which the Matron of Chartres had innocently aroused in me, rose out
of the past" (175). And, for the first time, Lewis wondered about a connection
between the longing for Joy and the desire for the occult.

Lewis had a profound experience of Joy while at Great Bookham, and it was as far from the occult as it could be; it was an experience he would come to recognize as holiness. The occasion was reading George MacDonald's *Phantastes: A Fairie Romance*. This experience of Joy, unlike previous ones, enhanced rather than diminished the world around him: "Up till now each visitation of Joy had left the common world momentarily a desert. . . . But now I saw the bright shadow coming out of the book into the real world and resting there, transforming all common things" (181). This Joy not only transformed Lewis's outer world but also his inner world, as evidenced in Lewis's Introduction to *George MacDonald: An Anthology*:

> [T]he whole book had about it a sort of cool, morning innocence, and also, quite unmistakably, a certain quality of Death, *good* Death. What it actually did to me was to convert, even to baptise (that was where the Death came in) my imagination. (MacDonald 1970: 21)

Between the time Lewis purchased *Phantastes* on March 4, 1916, and his nineteenth birthday, November 29, 1917, he finished his studies with Kirkpatrick, won a scholarship from University College, Oxford, trained for the military, and arrived on the frontlines in France as a second lieutenant. This was a world of death, "horribly smashed men still moving like half-crushed beetles," and desolation, "the landscape of sheer earth without a blade of grass" (Lewis 1955b: 196), the exact opposite of *Phantastes'* bright-shadowy world. Writing to Arthur Greeves in May and June of 1918, Lewis sketched a view Adam Barkman characterized as "Pseudo-Manichean-Dualism" (2009: 30–34) and David Downing described as "almost Manichean, insisting that Spirit and Matter existed in a state of perpetual opposition" (2002: 92):

> You will be surprised and I expect, not a little amused to hear that my views at present are getting almost monastic about all the lusts of the flesh. They seem to me to extend the dominion of matter over us: and, out here, where I see spirit continually dodging matter (shells, bullets, animal fears, animal pains) I have formulated my equation Matter = Nature = Satan. And on the other side Beauty, the only spiritual & not-natural thing I have yet found. (Lewis 2004a: 371)

> I believe in no God, least of all in one who would punish me for the "lusts of the flesh": but I do believe that I have in me a spirit, a chip, shall we say, of universal spirit; and that, since all good & joyful things are spiritual & non-material, I must be careful not to let matter (= nature = Satan, remember) get too great a hold on me, & dull the one spark I have. (379)

A world war later, Lewis gave broadcasts on the BBC, offering critiques of dualism (2001b: 4–5). He showed that referring to one side as evil and the other as good required a standard more fundamental than either side, thus depriving the competing sides of their status as ultimate reality (43).

When Lewis returned to Oxford after the war, he no longer affirmed the "spiritual & nonmaterial." His "'New Look' ... adopting a turn of phrase from the world of fashion and applying it to the intellectual trends of his day, as he chose to appropriate them" (McGrath 2014: 32) combined: materialistic monism (metaphysics), empiricism (epistemology), Stoicism (ethics), a debunking psychology, and "chronological snobbery." As a monist, Lewis believed that the material universe is all that exists. Joy now was merely an aesthetic experience, "But it came very seldom and when it came it didn't amount to much" (Lewis 1955b: 205). As an empiricist, he accepted "as rock-bottom reality the universe revealed by the senses" (208). If Bergson was right – and Lewis thought he was – the universe exists necessarily, and "There is no sense in blaming or praising the Whole.... . since you are part of it" (204). What is called for is acceptance, hence Stoicism. Influenced by the "New Psychology," Lewis now considered the romantic images he had once valued as so much "wishful thinking"; he had "seen through" them, and "was never going to be taken in again" (204). As a chronological snob, Lewis assumed that "whatever has gone out of date is on that account discredited" (207).

Lewis's good friend, Owen Barfield, did not like the look of Lewis's new fashion statement. Barfield found holes in Lewis's chronological snobbery. He claimed that before dismissing an earlier view, "You must find why it went out of date. Was it ever refuted (and if so by whom, where, and how conclusively) or did it merely die away as fashions do? If the latter, this tells us nothing about its truth or falsehood" (207–8). Worse yet, Barfield showed Lewis that in accepting "as rock-bottom reality the universe revealed by the senses," Lewis had to *either* give up his views that "abstract thought (if obedient to logical rules) gave indisputable truth, that our moral judgment was 'valid,' and our aesthetic experience not merely pleasing but 'valuable,'" *or* "adopt a Behavioristic theory of logic, ethics, and aesthetics" (208). Lewis was not willing to give up the objectivity of thought and pronounced himself unable to accept Behaviorism: "I cannot force my thought into that shape any more than I can scratch my ear with my big toe" (209). His only alternative was hitherto unthinkable: "I must admit that ... the whole universe was, in the last resort, mental; that our logic was participation in a cosmic *Logos*" (209).

Lewis had moved from an initial belief in "atoms and evolution" to idealism. He then explored two different forms of idealism: subjective and absolute. He initially turned to George Berkeley's (1685–1753) subjective idealism. On this view, all that exists are minds – first and foremost the divine mind – and their ideas. Lewis dropped this position when he saw that it could not account for interaction between finite minds (Barkman 2009: 224), and turned to the absolute idealism of F. H. Bradley (1846–1924). Michael L. Peterson summarizes Bradley's view:

> [R]eality is mind-coordinated and that both the intangibles of consciousness and the tangible objects of sensory experience are dependent on one mind, "the Absolute." Bradley's argument was that the notion of a multiplicity of separate objects which constitute reality is incoherent – and therefore that the Absolute, or Reality, *is* the totality of all Appearances. (2020: 24–25)

Adam Barkman notes that Lewis referred to F. H. Bradley as a "British Hegelian" and to G. F. W. Hegel (1770–1831) as a pantheist (2009: 46): "Bradley's absolute idealism, which focuses on the conditions for an intelligible world, is really no different than pantheism, which focuses on religion, since both doctrines would agree that everything is God" (46). Lewis had now shifted from subjective idealism to pantheism.

Pantheism, like subjective idealism, would turn out to be just another way station, but – for the time being – a pleasant one, comfort without cost:

> The Absolute differs from God much as a book differs from a friend; it is always there when you want it, but it will never bother you when you do not. It had all the charm of the occult without its terrors. It could excite, but not terrify. It could divinely comfort but not divinely rebuke. It would never, never interfere. (Lewis 2013: 31)

After his conversion, Lewis compared and contrasted Christianity and pantheism in "The Rival Conceptions of God" 2001b: 35–39) and "Christianity and 'Religion'" (Lewis 2001c: 129–50).

2.4 Two Conversions

Lewis had come a long way from his New Look. Any remaining detritus was "annihilated" (1955b: 217) when he reread Euripides's *Hippolytus*: "I was off once more into the land of longing, my heart at once broken and exalted as it had never been since the old days at Bookham [where Lewis read *Phantastes*]. There was nothing whatever to do about it; no question of returning to the desert" (217). Reading Samuel Alexander's Gifford Lectures *Space, Time, and Deity* gave Lewis a new understanding of this longing. He saw that "one essential property of love, hate, fear, hope, or desire was attention to their object" (218). From Alexander, Lewis learned that one cannot both experience love, hate, hope or the like, and reflect on that experience simultaneously: "You cannot hope and also think about hoping at the same moment; for in hope we look to hope's object and we interrupt this by (so to speak) turning round to look at the hope itself" (218). When Lewis made the connection with Joy, he realized that he had been on a fool's errand:

> This discovery flashed a new light back on my whole life. I saw that all my waitings and watchings for Joy, all my vain hopes to find some mental content on which I could, so to speak, lay my finger and say, "This is it," had been a futile attempt to contemplate the enjoyed. (219)

In looking inside himself to attend to a mental state that can only exist unattended to, and in looking inside himself to find the object of a desire that exists outside himself, Lewis's approach was self-defeating. He now knew that – properly approached – Joy provides "a road right out of the self" (221).

With a new understanding and experience of Joy, and a different philosophical framework (absolute idealism/pantheism), Lewis saw the possibility of a confluence:

> We mortals, seen as the sciences see us and as we commonly see one another, are mere "appearances." But appearances of the Absolute ... we have, so to speak, a root in the Absolute which is the utter reality. And that is why we experience Joy: we yearn, rightly, for that unity which we can never reach except by ceasing to be the separate phenomenal beings called "we." (221–22)

In the 1924–25 academic year, when Lewis was tutoring in philosophy, he hit a pedagogical wall: "A tutor must make things clear. Now the Absolute cannot be made clear" (222). Lewis chose to circumvent the wall by shifting back to Berkeley's subjective idealism, a form of theism. The move was pedagogically sound but personally troubling; Lewis wished to distance himself from the religious connotations of subjective idealism, and so referred to Berkeley's God as "Spirit," and emphasized the impossibility of having a personal relationship with it.

Although Lewis wished to keep matters philosophical and impersonal, more than a few factors threatened his wish. Among them were: an atheist colleague's reflection that the historicity of the gospels looked pretty good – maybe there had been a dying and rising god (Heck 2021: 213–17; Lewis 1955b: 223–24); Lewis's sense that he had been holding something "at bay," and needed to decide whether or not to keep the door shut (Lewis 1955b: 224); and a realization that, contrary to the great philosophers, Lewis had been treating philosophy merely as a subject, when it was in fact a way of life (225–26). When Lewis decided to open the door and live his philosophy, he became – not a Christian – but a theist "pure and simple" (230).

Lewis's turn to Christianity came later, after a long conversation with J.R.R. Tolkien and Hugo Dyson that began on September 19, 1931 and spilled over into the next day. Tolkien reflected on that evening in his poem, *Mythopoeia*, dedicating it to "one who said that myths were lies and therefore worthless, even though 'breathed through silver'" (J.R.R. Tolkien 1988: 85). Tolkien's son Christopher later noted that his father was referring to C.S. Lewis (C. Tolkien 1988: vii).

Tolkien countered Lewis's characterization with an image of his own, "refracted light."

> Though now long estranged,
> man is not wholly lost nor wholly changed.
> ... man, sub-creator, the refracted light
> through whom is splintered from a single White
> to many hues, and endlessly combined
> in living shapes that move from mind to mind. (J. Tolkien 1988: 87)

There are echoes of Tolkien's poem in Lewis's description of myth in *Miracles*, "at its best, a real though unfocused gleam of divine truth falling on human imagination" (2001c: 218).

Lewis gave his own account of the evening in his letters to Arthur Greeves on October 1 and 18, 1931:

> Now what Dyson and Tolkien showed me was this: that if I met the idea of sacrifice in a Pagan story I didn't mind it at all ... I liked it very much and was mysteriously moved by it: again, that the idea of the dying and reviving god (Balder, Adonis, Bacchus) similarly moved me provided I met it anywhere *except* in the Gospels. (2004a: 976–77)

> Now the story of Christ is simply a true myth: a myth working on us in the same way as the others, but with this tremendous difference that *it really happened*. (977)

> I have just passed on from believing in God to definitely believing in Christ – in Christianity.... My long night talk with Dyson and Tolkien had a good deal to do with it. (974)

Lewis's long journey that began with a toy garden in a biscuit tin and his mother's death, culminated in belief in Christ.

For Further Reading: Two works chronicle Lewis's conversion to Christianity (Downing 2002; Heck 2017). Another (Brown 2013) takes a longer look at Lewis's spiritual journey, encompassing his entire life. On the dating of Lewis's conversion, see Alister McGrath's groundbreaking work (McGrath 2013: 141–46). Lewis's semi-autobiographical, allegorical conversion account, *The Pilgrim's Regress*, is a challenging work; the Wade Center's annotated edition is a valuable resource (Lewis 2014). Michael L. Peterson offers a lucid account of Lewis's "worldview journey" (2020:15–30). For a detailed account of Lewis's philosophical development see Adam Barkman (2009: 11–213). Harry Lee Poe's Biographical Trilogy (2019, 2021, 2022) provides a thorough account of Lewis's entire life. Joel Heck's chronology of the lives of C.S. Lewis and Warren Lewis is an invaluable resource (2022b).

3 The Case for Theism

3.1 An Ontological Argument in Narnia?

The Silver Chair, one of The Chronicles of Narnia, introduces Puddleglum, a character who takes pessimism to new lows. Notwithstanding his gloomy outlook – it is not for nothing that his name ends in "glum" – he turns out to be a hero: he stomps out the Queen of Underland's enchanted fire, breaking her spell. It is clear from one of Lewis's letters that he took this episode in *The Silver Chair* to be philosophically significant:

> I suppose your philosopher son – what a family you have been privileged to bring into the world! – means the chapter in which Puddleglum put out the fire with his foot. He must thank Anselm and Descartes for it, not me. I have simply put the "Ontological Proof'" in a form suitable for children. (2007: 1472)

Lest the philosophical import escape us, Walter Hooper provides some commentary:

> The ontological proof or ontological argument comes originally from the Proslogion of St. Anselm of Canterbury (1033–1109) and can be formulated as follows: (1) "God" is the greatest being which can be thought. (2) It is greater to exist in reality and in thought than in thought alone. (3) Therefore, "God" exists in reality and in thought. (1472)

> Lewis has Puddleglum use the ontological proof in *The Silver Chair*, chapter 12. The Queen of Underland argues that "You can put nothing into your make-believe without copying it from the real world, which . . . is the only world." "Suppose," answers Puddleglum, "we have only dreamed or made up, all those things – trees and grass and sun and moon and stars and Aslan himself. Suppose we have. Then all I can say is that, in that case, the made-up things seem a good deal more important than the real ones . . . We're just babies making up a game, if you're right. But four babies playing a game can make a play-world which licks your real world hollow. (1472)

Here Hooper uncharacteristically falters. He conflates Anselm's *a priori* conceptual approach with an *a posteriori* matter, a causal question over the origin of ideas. Anselm, as represented by Hooper, is arguing from the supposition that God is the greatest being which can be thought, to God's existence. Anselm is not concerned with the question, *Where did our idea of God come from?* But a question like *Where did Puddleglum's idea of Aslan come from?* is at the heart of the dispute between the Queen of Underland and Puddleglum. They are not concerned with conceptual questions along the lines of *Given the supposition that Aslan is king of the beasts, can we infer that Aslan exists?*

In addition to the mismatch between the approaches in *The Proslogion* and *The Silver Chair,* there is another reason for supposing that, *pace* Hooper, Lewis did not have in mind Anselm's conceptual proof of God's existence: Lewis dismissed the possibility of such proofs and appealed to the explanatory power of the Christian worldview in their place:

> As for proof, I sometimes wonder whether the Ontological Argument did not itself arise as a partially unsuccessful translation of an experience without concepts or words. I don't think we can initially argue from the *concept* of Perfect Being to its existence (Lewis 1967a, p. 141).

> I do not think there is a *demonstrative proof* (like Euclid) of Christianity, nor of the existence of matter, nor of the good will & honesty of my best & oldest friends. I think all three are (except perhaps the second) far more probable than the alternatives. (Lewis 2007: 1950)

> Christian theology can fit in science, art, morality, and the sub–Christian religions. The scientific point of view cannot fit in any of these things, not even science itself. I believe in Christianity as I believe that the sun has risen, not only because I see it, but because by it, I see everything else (Lewis 1980: 92)

While Lewis identified both Anselm and Descartes as originators of the "Ontological Proof" (Lewis's scare quotes) in *The Silver Chair* passage, he did not point to any specific passages. However, his comments on a Cartesian proof in a letter to his brother seem pertinent:

> Yes indeed: how many essays I have heard read to me on Descartes's proofs (there are more than one) of the existence of God. . . . The particular one you quote ("I have an idea of a perfect being") seems to me to be valid or invalid according to the meaning you give the words "have an idea of." I used to work it out by the analogy of a machine. If I have the idea of a machine which I, being unmechanical, couldn't have invented on my own, does this prove that I have received the idea from some really mechanical source – e.g. a talk with the real inventor? To which I answer "Yes" if you mean a really detailed idea. (Lewis 2004b: 7)

In his editorial notes on this letter, Walter Hooper correctly identifies the relevant Cartesian argument:

In the third of his *Meditations on First Philosophy*, Descartes's argument for the existence of God runs: "I have the idea of a perfect being. Whatever *caused* this idea must have all the perfections represented in the idea." (7)

Keeping Lewis's letter to his brother in mind, recall Puddleglum's response to the Queen of Underland:

"Suppose we *have* only dreamed, or made up, all those things – trees and grass and sun and moon and stars and Aslan himself. Suppose we have. . . . Suppose this black pit of a kingdom of yours *is* the only world. Well, it strikes me as a pretty poor one. And that's a funny thing, when you come to think of it. We're just babies making up a game, if you're right. But four babies playing a game can make a play-world which licks your real world hollow." (Lewis 2000b: 182)

We can easily express the reasoning implicit in Puddleglum's remarks in the form of a Cartesian argument: Puddleglum has the idea of a world of light and beauty. He, being a "baby," could not have invented that idea if the Queen's "black pit" had been the only world he knew. So, it seems that Puddleglum received his ideas either from a world filled with sunlight or from someone who knew of such a world. There is, then, good reason to think that Descartes' causal proof in the Third Meditation is the "Ontological Proof" (Lewis's scare quotes) that Lewis gave "in a form suitable for children" in *The Silver Chair*.

For Further Reading: For a different interpretation of *The Silver Chair* passage and the ontological argument, see Donald T. Williams (2016: 75–80). McGrath (2014: 129–46) discusses Lewis's apologetic approach.

3.2 The Moral Argument

C.S. Lewis once remarked to his friend Neville Coghill, "I *believe* I have proved that the Renaissance never happened in England. *Alternatively* . . . that if it did, *it had no importance*" (Coghill 1965: 61). It was fitting, then, for Cambridge University to offer Lewis a chair in Medieval and Renaissance Literature, which led Lewis to conclude that Cambridge "was encouraging my own belief that the barrier between those two ages has been greatly exaggerated" (Lewis 1979: 2). In his inaugural address "*De Descriptione Temporum,*" Lewis focused on what he took to be a much deeper division: "I have come to regard as the greatest of all divisions in the history of the West that which divides the present from, say, the age of Jane Austen [1775–1817] and Scott [1771–1832]" (7); "In her [Jane Austen's] days some kind and degree of religious belief and practice were the norm: now, though . . . they are the exception" (9–10).

Lewis saw the present age as post-Christian and considered Paganism preferable to it, as early Christian missionaries had an advantage over evangelists to post-Christians:

> The earliest missionaries, the Apostles, preached to three sorts of men: to Jews, to those Judaizing Gentiles ... and to Pagans. In all three classes they could count on certain predispositions which we cannot count on in our audience. All three classes believed in the Supernatural ... All were conscious of sin and divine judgment. (1986a: 61)

> The idea ... that Christianity brought a new ethical code into the world is a grave error. If it had done so ... its Founder, His precursor, His apostles, came demanding repentance and offering forgiveness, a demand and an offer both meaningless except on the assumption of a moral law already known and already broken. (Lewis 1967a: 46)

Aware that his war-time broadcast audience was post-Christian, Lewis set out to make Christianity meaningful by starting off with reflections on the moral law. In adducing evidence for an objective moral law, Lewis noted that quarreling presupposes a shared moral standard (Lewis 2001b: 3–4); a denial of such a standard leads to an absurdity: "What was the sense in saying the enemy were in the wrong unless Right is a real thing which the Nazis at bottom knew as well as we did and ought to have practiced?" (5); moral differences across cultures have been exaggerated (1955a: 95–121; 2001b: 6); and mistaken moral beliefs no more undermine the objectivity of morality than do errors in mathematics (Lewis 2001b: 7). Following these considerations, Lewis addressed some objections: the moral law is just "herd instinct," (9–12) or social convention (12–14). Satisfied that he had made his case, Lewis concluded that there is a moral law, which differs from the laws of nature in that it does not merely report what is, but expresses what ought to be. It is "a real law, which none of us made, but which we feel pressing on us" (20), "which we know we ought to obey" (21).

Taking the reality of the moral law as a datum, Lewis then considered its implications for deciding between two opposing philosophies: the materialist view and the religious view:

> People who take that view [the materialist view] think that matter and space just happen to exist, and always have existed, nobody knows why; and that the matter, behaving in certain fixed ways, has just happened, by a sort of fluke, to produce creatures like ourselves who are able to think. ... According to it [the religious view], what is behind the universe is more like a mind than it is like anything else we know. That is to say, it is conscious, and has purposes, and prefers one thing to another. And on this view it made the universe, partly ... at any rate, in order to produce creatures like itself – I mean, like itself to the extent of having minds. (21–22)

In favor of a fit between the reality of the moral law and the religious view, Lewis argued that since our knowledge of morality cannot come, as does scientific knowledge, from the third-person perspective, it must be known from the first-person perspective:

> We do not merely observe men, we *are* men. In this case we have, so to speak, inside information; we are in the know. And because of that, we know that men find themselves under a moral law, which they did not make, and cannot quite forget even when they try, and which they know they ought to obey. (23)

Such "inside information" is just what we would expect were the religious view true:

> If there was a controlling power outside of the universe, it could not show itself to us as one of the facts inside the universe – no more than an architect of a house could actually be a wall or a staircase . . . in that house. The only way in which we could expect it to show itself would be inside ourselves as an influence or command trying to get us to behave in a certain way. And that is just what we do find inside ourselves. (24)

In contrast, the materialist view – relying on science – cannot tell us whether or not there is something more than the physical universe, for questions like that lie beyond the purview of science (23), and do not offer us much hope for confidence in our moral convictions. For on this view, it is only "by a very long series of chances, the living creatures developed into things like us" (22). As Lewis saw it, the result of comparing the religious and materialist views on the reality of the moral law pointed to "Something which is directing the universe, and which appears in me as a law urging me to do right. . . . is more like a mind than it is like anything else we know" (25). It is important to keep Lewis's moral argument in perspective. If successful, he has shown that the religious view is preferable to strict materialism in accounting for our knowledge of the moral law. Whether or not this is so for a broader form of naturalism is another matter (Taliaferro 2010: 111–12). And, as Lewis was aware, there are other phenomena to consider, not least our desire for heaven and our ability to make rational inferences.

For Further Reading: See Baggett and Walls (2019: 162–80) for a discussion of Lewis's moral arguments, and the exemplary exchange between Wielenberg, con (2015a; 2015b) and Baggett, pro (2015a; 2015b). C.S. Lewis argued for the objectivity of morality in *The Abolition of Man* (1955a); Michael Ward's guide (2021) is an essential resource for that work. Jerry Root shows that "Lewis believed subjectivism, left unchecked, leads to evil" (2009: 1)

3.3 The Argument from Desire

Augustine addressed God, "You have made us for yourself and our hearts find no peace until they rest in You" (1961:21). Pascal wrote about an "infinite abyss" that "can be filled only with an infinite and immutable object, in other words by God himself" (1966: 75). And C.S. Lewis described "a desire which no experience in this world can satisfy," (Lewis 2001a: 136–37), a longing where "the sense of want is acute and even painful, yet the mere wanting of it is felt somehow to be a delight" (Lewis 1958b: 7), and "our lifelong nostalgia" (Lewis 1980: 12). The richness and complexity of this desire is apparent in the variety of terms Lewis used to characterize it: Platonic *Eros*; Romanticism; the *Numinous*; *Sehnsucht*; Joy; and Hope (Barkman 2009: 67–86). In *Mere Christianity* Lewis referred to the desire's object as "Heaven" (2001b: 135), "infinite happiness" (136), and "my true country" (137). In "The Weight of Glory" he referred to it as "a transtemporal, transfinite good" (Lewis 1980: 6), "our longing to be united with something in the universe from which we now feel cut off" (16), and "freshness and purity" (17). The importance of this transfinite good cannot be overemphasized. If there were no such good, the universe would be a fraud (Lewis 2001b: 137); but if there were such a good, then "If we lose this, we lose all" (Lewis 2001d: 151). Nothing less is at stake than the meaningfulness of life (Goetz 2018: 174; Peterson, Michael L. 2020: 43–6; Wielenberg 2008: 111; Williams, Peter S. 2015a: 44).

Lewis never offered a formal argument from desire for infinite happiness. And, when he did discuss the significance of desire, he assessed it differently. He used the language of probability in "The Weight of Glory": "I think it is a pretty good indication that such a thing exists" (1980: 6), and in *Mere Christianity:* "Probably earthly pleasures were never meant to satisfy it" (2001b: 137). But in *The Pilgrim's Regress,* Lewis was more emphatic: "the One who can sit in this chair must exist" (1958b: 10). If nature does nothing in vain, the object of the desire "must" exist:

> It appeared to me therefore that if a man diligently followed this desire, pursuing the false objects until their falsity appeared and then resolutely abandoning them, he must come out at last into the clear knowledge that the human soul was made to enjoy some object that is never fully given ... in our present mode of subjective and spatio-temporal experience. This Desire was, in the soul, as the Siege Perilous in Arthur's castle – the chair in which only one could sit. And if nature makes nothing in vain, the One who can sit in this chair must exist. (10)

As Lewis used both the language of demonstrative certainty, "must," and probability, Lewis scholars have formalized his reasoning from desire to infinite good in a variety of ways: Abductive (McGrath 2014: 117–120); Inference to the best explanation (John Haldane inMcGrath 2014: 120–2; Williams, Donald 2017; Williams, Peter S. 2015a); Bayesian (Simek 2022); Inductive (Beversluis 2007: 43; Hoyler 1988: 68–70); Deductive (Beversluis 2007: 41; Kreeft 1989: 250; Williams, Peter S. 2015a: 41); "Deductive with epistemic qualifiers" (Lee 2017: 324–25); Reductio argument from absurdity (Lovell 2003: 139–45; Williams, Peter S. 2015a: 43–44).

In order to clarify and consider some of the issues Lewis's argument raises, it will be helpful to have an explicit version of the argument before us. The following is from Peter Kreeft:

> The major premise of the argument is that *every natural desire or innate desire in us bespeaks a corresponding real object that can satisfy the desire.* The minor premise is *there exists in us a desire which nothing in time, nothing on earth, no creature, can satisfy.* The conclusion is that *there exists something outside of time, earth, and creatures which can satisfy this desire.* (Kreeft 1989: 250)

Note that in the major premise, there is an implied distinction between natural/innate desires and external desires. John Haldane provides the following characterization of natural/innate desires:

> 1) Spontaneity of occurrence; 2) prevalence to the extent of normal universality; and 3) common linguistic identification of types of desire and/or of their satisfaction, and/or of their deprivation. The desire for food and sex occur without cultivation; are prevalent to the extent that their absence generally invites explanation; and natural languages have words for these desires and/or for their fulfilment and/or their frustration. (quoted in Simek 2022)

By way of clarification, Lewis notes that from the fact that there is such an object for every natural desire, it follows only that every natural desire can be satisfied, not that every one *will* be satisfied. We have a natural desire for food, yet some starve.

The minor premise presupposes that the desire for heaven/infinite happiness is universal. Even so, Lewis realizes that some may miss it: "when the real want for Heaven is present in us, we do not recognize it. Most people if they had really learned to look into their hearts, would know and know that they want, and want acutely. Something that cannot be had in this world" (Lewis 2001b: 135). The key is knowing how to look. If we look at our desires only from a third-person point of view, the results will be reductionistic and leave us with knowledge of neural pathways. If we look at our desires from the first-person point of view, we will see that they are teleological and point beyond themselves. This is the distinction Lewis drew between "looking at" (third-person perspective) and "looking along" (first-person perspective) in "Meditation in a Toolshed." Looking at a beam of light coming in through a crack in the toolshed, we see "specks of dust floating in it" (Lewis 1970: 212). Looking along the beam, we see "green leaves moving on the branches of a tree outside and beyond that, ninety odd million miles away, the sun" (212).

For Further Reading: For different perspectives on Lewis's argument from desire, see the exchange between Peter S. Williams, pro (2015a; 2015b; 2016) and Gregory Bassham, con (2015a; 2015b) as well as Erik J. Wielenberg's critique (2008: 116–17) and Stewart Goetz's "Lewisian" response (2018: 174–77). McGrath (2019) compares the views of C.S. Lewis and Richard Dawkins on the meaning of life.

3.4 The Argument from Reason

On March 11, 1936, Lewis wrote a fan letter to Charles Williams:

> I have just read your *Place of the Lion* and it is to me one of the major literary events of my life – comparable to my first discovery of George McDonald, G. K. Chesterton, or Wm. Morris. There are layers and layers – first the pleasure that any good fantasy gives me . . . Combined with this, the pleasure of a real philosophical and theological stimulus. . . . Honestly, I didn't think there was anyone now alive in England who could do it. (Lewis 2004b: 183)

In *The Place of the Lion* (1950), Williams' protagonist Damaris Tighe (her first name appears in Acts 17:34), studies Plato and Aristotle but fails to see the significance of events – the return of Archetypes – in the world around her. Lewis thought that naturalist philosophers have the opposite problem; they fail to perceive the significance of the events within them: "The Naturalists have been engaged in thinking about Nature. They have not attended to the fact that they were *thinking*" Lewis (2001c: 65).

Lewis took it for granted that self-reflection shows that we make rational inferences, and if we arrive at theories only through such inferences, then any theory that rules them out is self-refuting:

> A theory which explained everything else in the whole universe but which made it impossible to believe that our thinking was valid, would be utterly out of court. For that theory would itself have been reached by thinking, and if thinking is not valid that theory would, of course, be itself demolished. It would have destroyed its own credentials. (21–22)

By way of example, Lewis quoted J.B. Haldane to show that "strict materialism" is self-refuting: "'If my mental processes are determined wholly by the motions of atoms in my brain, I have no reason to suppose that my beliefs are true ... and hence I have no reason for supposing my brain to be composed of atoms'" (quoted in 2001c: 22).

"Strict materialism" is but one form of naturalism. In general, "The Naturalist believes that a great process, of 'becoming', exists 'on its own' in space and time, and that nothing else exists" (12), and that whatever occurs is "an inevitable result of the character of the whole system" (15). Note that Lewis's account of naturalism does not rule out the existence of minds: "The great interlocking event called Nature might be such as to produce at some stage a great cosmic consciousness, an indwelling 'God' arising from the whole process as human mind arises (according to the Naturalists) from human organisms" (11). However, minds that are the inevitable result of an entirely naturalistic system cannot accommodate reasoning:

> It is agreed on all hands that reason, and even sentience, and life itself are late comers in Nature. If there is nothing but Nature, therefore, reason must have come into existence by a historical process. And of course, for the Naturalist, this process was not designed to produce a mental behaviour that can find truth. There was no Designer.... The type of mental behaviour we call rational thinking or inference must therefore have "evolved" by natural selection. (27)

> Now natural selection could operate only by eliminating responses that were biologically hurtful and multiplying those which tended to survival. But it is not conceivable that any improvement of responses could ever turn them into acts of insight.... The relation between response and stimulus is utterly different from that between knowledge and the truth known. (28)

Central to Lewis's critique of naturalism, whether natural selection or strict materialism, is his principle that "a train of thought loses all rational credentials as soon as it can be shown to be wholly the result of non-rational causes" (Lewis 2001c: 39). Note the qualification "wholly": "the argument from reason does not require that our cognitive functioning be completely unaffected by physical causes, evolutionary or otherwise" (Peterson 2020: 55). So, if we make rational inferences, there must be a sense in which each of us is "a more than natural agent" (2001c: 177). As such, if a miracle is "an interference with Nature by supernatural power" (5), then our reasoning is – in some sense – miraculous and hints at "the grand miracle," the incarnation:

> What can be meant by "God becoming man"? In what sense is it conceivable that eternal self–existent Spirit, basic Fact-hood, should be so combined with a natural human organism as to make one person? And this would be a fatal stumbling block if we had not already discovered in every human being a more than natural activity (the act of reasoning) and therefore presumably a more than natural agent is thus united with a part of Nature: so united that the composite creature calls itself "I" and "Me." (176–77)

For Further Reading: C.S. Lewis encountered the argument from reason in Arthur Balfour's *Theism and Humanism* (2000). Taliaferro (2015) provides an overview of Balfour's work and contrasts it with the work of influential contemporary philosophers. Lewis first offered the argument in *Miracles* (Lewis 1947: 23–32) and then recast it in the 1960 revised edition of *Miracles* (Lewis 2001c: 17–36). For Elizabeth Anscombe's critique of Lewis's first version of the argument see (Anscombe 1981: 224–32) and for her subsequent reflections, see (1981: ix-x). For her discussion of Lewis's revised argument, see (Anscombe 2015: 15–23). No one has done more to explicate, defend, and develop C.S. Lewis's argument from reason than Victor Reppert. Representative writings include: *C.S. Lewis's Dangerous Idea* (2003), and an exchange with David Kyle Johnson (Johnson 2015a, 2015b, 2018; Reppert 2015a, 2015b, 2018). Alvin Plantinga (2011: 310) sees his own evolutionary argument against naturalism as a descendent of Lewis's. For a comparison of the approaches of Plantinga and Lewis, see Goetz (2013) and Depoe (2014).

4 The Case for Christianity

4.1 The Myth Became Fact

Reflecting on his friendship with Arthur Greeves, Lewis wrote, "I learned charity from him and failed, for all my efforts, to teach him arrogance in return" (Lewis 2004a: 995). Lewis's conceit was on full display in his letter to Arthur on October 12, 1916:

> You ask me about my religious views: you know, I think I believe in no religion. There is absolutely no proof for any of them, and from a philosophical standpoint Christianity is not even the best. All religions, that is, all mythologies to give them their proper name are merely man's own invention – Christ as much as Loki. . . . Often, too, great men were regarded as gods after their death – such as Heracles or Odin: thus after the death of a Hebrew philosopher Yeshua (whose name we have corrupted into Jesus) he became regarded as a god . . . and so Christianity came into being – one mythology among many. (230–31)

On October 18, 1916, Lewis wrote Greeves to clarify comments in his previous letter:

> I distinctly said that there once was a Hebrew named Yeshua . . . when I say "Christ" of course I mean the mythological being into whom he was afterward converted by popular imagination, and I am thinking of the legends about his magic performances and resurrection etc. . . . all the other tomfoolery about virgin birth, magic healings, apparitions and so forth is on exactly the same footing as any other mythology. (234)

Lewis wrote these letters when William T. Kirkpatrick was his tutor. Kirkpatrick, once a believer, was at that time an atheist. "At the time when I knew him, the fuel of Kirk's Atheism was chiefly of the anthropological and pessimistic kind. He was great on *The Golden Bough* and Schopenhauer" (Lewis 1955b: 139).

Kirkpatrick did not convert Lewis to atheism – it was too late for that – but he did provide Lewis with "fresh ammunition" (140). Lewis's remarks to Arthur Greeves are in keeping with James Frazer's perspective in *The Golden Bough:*

> From *The Golden Bough*, a comprehensive work on comparative religions and mythology . . . Lewis came to feel that religion was simply an expression of culture, that all peoples had their own myths and legends, just as they had their own customs, and that no one system of beliefs, such as Christianity, was any more "true" than any other. (Downing 2002: 52)

A breakthrough in Lewis's understanding of myth and an openness to Christianity came through a conversation with J.R.R. Tolkien and Hugo Dyson. Lewis shared the lessons he learned from Dyson and Tolkien in a letter to Arthur Greeves, written fifteen years to the day after his October 18, 1916 "tomfoolery letter":

> Now what Dyson and Tolkien showed me was this: that if I met the idea of sacrifice in a Pagan story I didn't mind it at all: again, that if I met the idea of a god sacrificing himself to himself . . . I liked it very much and was mysteriously moved by it: again, that the idea of the dying and reviving god (Balder, Adonis, Bacchus) similarly moved me provided I met it anywhere *except* in the Gospels. . . . Now the story of Christ is a true myth a myth working on us in the same way as others, but with the tremendous difference that it *really happened*. (Lewis 2004a: 976–77)

Taking his cue from Tolkien and Dyson, Lewis eventually moved from seeing the presence of parallels between Christianity and nature religions as problematic to the position that their absence would be worrisome:

> I could not believe Christianity if I were forced to say that there were a thousand religions in the world of which 999 were pure nonsense and the thousandth (fortunately) true. (Lewis 1970: 132)

> We must not be ashamed of the mythical radiance resting on our theology. We must not be nervous about "parallels" and "Pagan Christs": they *ought* to be there – it would be a stumbling block if they weren't. (67)

The pattern of death and rebirth occurs in nature religions because the natural world is God's creation: "The pattern is there in Nature because it was first there in God" (Lewis 2001c: 181). Christ "from all eternity has been incessantly plunging Himself in the blessed death of self-surrender to the Father" (211). And, since God provides "the true light which enlightens everyone" (John 1:9 ESV),

> We should, therefore, expect to find in the imagination of great Pagan teachers and myth makers some glimpse of that theme which we believe to be the very plot of the whole cosmic story – the theme of incarnation, death, and rebirth. (Lewis 1980: 83)

These glimpses were *"preparatio evangelica"* (Lewis 1970: 132) before religion had reached its maturity (Lewis 1955b: 235). When religion finally matured in Christianity, the "elements of Nature-religion are strikingly absent from the teaching of Jesus," for "Where the real God is present the shadows of that God do not appear" (Lewis 2001c: 186). That the Christian story can account for both the presence and absence of "shadows," counts strongly in its favor: "The truth of a given worldview ... is in its ability not to fit into other myths, but its ability to 'fit in' the other myths into its own story" (Honeycut 2017: 117).

Lewis argued that "the Grand Miracle" (2001c: 174), the doctrine of the incarnation, explained more than "parallels" and "Pagan Christs" (1970: 67). Among other things, it elucidated the vicariousness found in nature: "Everything is indebted to everything else, sacrificed to everything else, dependent on everything else" (Lewis 2001c: 191), and "the composite nature of man" (191). In general, for Lewis, the credibility of the doctrine "will depend upon the extent to which the doctrine, if accepted, can illuminate and integrate that whole mass [of our knowledge]" (176).

For Further Reading: Those interested in reflecting on the ways Lewis's view of myth can integrate and illuminate the collective unconscious may wish to peruse "Synthesizing True Myth and Jungian Criticism: Jordan Peterson, Carl Jung, and C.S. Lewis in Conversation" (Trudeau 2021). For a comparison of the views of C.S. Lewis and James Campbell, see (Menzies 2014), and for a broader and briefer introduction (Hyles 1992).

4.2 More than a Great Moral Teacher

Throughout his writings, Lewis contrasted descriptions of Jesus's claims about himself with his moral teaching: *The Problem of Pain* (2001d: 13); "What Are We To Make of Jesus Christ?" (1970: 156); *Mere Christianity* (2001b: 51–52):

> The historical difficulty of giving for the life, sayings and influence of Jesus any explanation that is not harder than the Christian explanation, is very great. The discrepancy between the depth and sanity (and let me add) *shrewdness* of his moral teaching and the rampant megalomania which must be behind his theological teaching unless he is indeed God, has never been satisfactorily gotten over. (Lewis 2001c: 174)

Elaborating on this apparent megalomania, Lewis noted that Jesus claimed "to be, or to be the son of, or to be 'one with,' the Something which is at once the awful haunter of nature and the giver of the moral law" (Lewis 2001d: 13); acted as if "He really was the God whose laws are broken and whose love is wounded in every sin" (Lewis 2001b: 52); asserted that he can forgive sins (51); "that His mere presence suspends all normal rules" and stated that "before Abraham was, I am" (1970: 157); and "denied all sin of Himself" (Lewis 1986b: 135), all the while describing himself as "meek and lowly of heart" (135).

In *Mere Christianity*, C.S. Lewis argued that Jesus's exalted claims would have been false only if he were either a liar or a lunatic. However, if we assume – as Lewis did – that Jesus was a great moral teacher, then the liar and lunatic options are off the table. The only remaining possibility is that Jesus was God incarnate.

Friends and foes of Lewis's line of reasoning agree that Lewis's three options do not exhaust the possibilities. Indeed, Lewis himself recognized that the possibility of legend needed to be addressed: "Something will usually have to be said about the historicity of the Gospels" (Lewis 1970: 101). In addition to the legend, lunatic, liar, and God incarnate possibilities, Alister McGrath suggests another: perhaps "Jesus was someone who was not mad or bad, but was nevertheless *wrong* about his identity" (McGrath 2013: 227). In keeping with McGrath's suggestion, John Beversluis makes a sharp distinction between the content of Jesus's teaching and the question of his identity:

> The question of whether Jesus' moral teachings are sound and the question of whether Jesus was God are separate questions and must be answered in logically independent ways. If it is not the metaphysical status of a moral teacher but the content of his teachings that make them sound ("sane," "deep," and so forth), then they remain sound ... *even if the teacher was mistaken about other matters.* (2007: 134)

Could Jesus have been mistaken about his identity – falsely believing himself to be divine, while giving sound moral instruction? This seems unlikely. Insofar as Jesus believed himself to be divine, he would have at least implicitly taught that the first and greatest commandment (to love the Lord your God with all of your heart, soul, mind, and might) applied to himself (cf. Bowman Jr. and Komoszewski 2007:31). Wrongly hinting, or worse, to others that their highest duty is to love you, is sufficient reason for exclusion from the class of great moral teachers.

Daniel Howard-Snyder believes that Jesus is divine, but thinks that it is possible that a merely human Jesus could have sufficient reasons for affirming his own divinity. In that case, Jesus would have been merely mistaken, albeit about a momentous matter. One way Howard-Synder offers support for this option is to sketch two possible scenarios. In one, the Beelzebub Story (473–75), Jesus is deceived by Satan. In the other, the Messianic Story, "first, Jesus came to believe he himself was Messiah ben David. Then, given his reading of the Jewish Scriptures, he came to believe that Messiah was divine. He made the natural deduction" (477).

Note that in order to establish the merely-mistaken option, it is not enough to provide possible scenarios. One must show that given one or both of these scenarios, "it is no less plausible to suppose that Jesus was neither mad nor bad but merely mistaken than that he was divine" (456). In response to Howard-Snyder's scenarios, Stephen T. Davis emphasizes that we should not lose sight of the fact that the Jesus in question is the one presented in the New Testament.

> It has never been my view that it is impossible to cook up scenarios in which a sane and moral person could mistakenly consider himself divine. But even for someone other than Jesus, it seems to me extremely difficult to make such a scenario plausible. And when we turn to Jesus – a person about whom we know a great deal (surely more than anyone else in the ancient world) – it seems to me that the difficulty increases geometrically.... The probability that Jesus was in such a scenario, i.e., was deluded to such a degree, will be so low as to be unworthy of serious scholarly consideration. It comes nowhere near squaring with the Jesus about whom we read in the New Testament. (487–88)

Whether or not these thought experiments square with the Jesus of the New Testament is left for the reader's reflection.

In an exchange with Donald S. Williams, Adam Barkman explores – without endorsing – one more possibility: in contrast to the conservative view in which Jesus is divine, and the liberal view in which he was "merely a wise man" (Barkman 2015a: 193) perhaps Jesus was neither divine nor human. Perhaps he was a different sort of being altogether, more than human but less than divine. In casting reasonable doubt on the conservative view that Jesus claimed to be God, Barkman rightly cautions about a tendency to "want to put difficult-to-classify entities [e.g. Jesus as the Son of Man] into easily identifiable boxes" (192). There is a danger of "seeing" more in a text than is actually there, as "Worship" (195); "Son of God" (Barkman 2015a: 196; Baynes 2017: 44–45); and "Son of Man" (Barkman 2015a: 194–7; Baynes 2017: 61–63) each has a range of meanings.

In trying to determine if, and to what extent, Jesus claimed to be divine, the "I am" sayings in the gospel of John are key texts. Barkman allows that they are among the sayings that "do support the traditional Trinitarian case but not as many – including, perhaps, Lewis – have thought" (197). Donald Williams, Barkman's interlocutor, is among the "many" who see "Before Abraham was I am" (John 8:58) as providing strong support for Jesus's claim to divinity.

Jesus here, in no uncertain terms, identifies his own ego, his "I," with that of
Jahweh. In a first-century Jewish context, a more brash and bold claim to
deity can hardly be imagined. And his contemporaries showed that they
understood this claim quite well: They attempted to stone him for blas-
phemy (John 8:59). The other titles should be read, not in isolation, but in
the context of the more unambiguous statements such as this one. (Williams
2015b: 202–3)

Barkman demurs. He argues that if Williams' reading of John 8 were right,
then every time Jesus used the expression "I am" there would be a similar
response.

Williams is certainly right that these statements could recall Exodus 3:14
(Yahweh's "I Am Who I Am"), but is this the best interpretation? If Jesus'
words were understood to allude to the Exodus passage, then we would have
expected them to provoke extreme outrage each time they were uttered.

However, in the other seven instances of "I am" that Barkman identifies (John
6:35, 8:12, 10:7, 10:11, 11:25, 14:6, 15:1), all of them metaphorical (e.g. "I am
the bread that came down from heaven"), none elicits a violent reaction.
Barkman concludes, "there is little evidence that Jesus' use of 'I am' statements
in John were either intended or understood to claim that he was God" (Barkman
2015b: 206). As for the crowd's reaction to "Before Abraham was, I am," he
advises,

Here it is important to understand the context, however. Jesus' statement
["Before Abraham was I am"] is the culmination of a long-running argument
with the Jews in which he declares that they are not true children of Abraham,
that their father is the devil, and that they will "die in [their] sins." (206)

Note that one could agree with Barkman regarding the evidential status of
Jesus's metaphorical uses of "I am," but part company with him on the significance of John 8:58 "as the one apparent exception." So, for example, Gary
Manning looks at John 8:58 together with John 6:19–20 and John 18: 6–8 and
draws an altogether different conclusion.

- They saw Jesus walking on the sea … and they were frightened. But he
  said to them,
  "It is I (ἐγώ εἰμι); do not be afraid." (John 6:19–20)
- "Truly, truly I say to you: before Abraham was, I am (ἐγώ εἰμι)." (John 8:58)
- Jesus said to [the soldiers], "Whom do you seek?" They answered "Jesus of
  Nazareth." Jesus answered "I am he (ἐγώ εἰμι)." … when Jesus said to
  them "I am he (ἐγώ εἰμι)," they retreated and fell to the ground … Jesus
  answered "I told you that I am he (ἐγώ εἰμι)." (John 18:6–8)

In each of these three, the context suggests that Jesus' deity is implied. In John 6:19, the phrase "walking on the sea" (περιπατοῦντα ἐπὶ τῆς θαλάσσης) is probably an allusion to God walking on the sea (περιπατῶν ... ἐπὶ θαλάσσης) in Job 9:8. Jesus' use of ἐγώ εἰμι and "do not be afraid" seems to further draw attention to his deity. In John 8:58, Jesus' description of his preexistence, combined with the bare ἐγώ εἰμι, is also clearly about his deity. The repetition of ἐγώ εἰμι in John 18:6–8, and its stunning effect on the soldiers, also implies Jesus' deity. (Manning 2015)

If Manning is correct, several "I am" statements in John's gospel were intended and/or understood to be claims to deity. Whether or not this is so, the interpretive issues surrounding Jesus's use of "I am" show that any credible assessment of Lewis's trilemma will depend upon very close readings of the relevant texts.

For Further Reading: Those interested in pursuing the historical reliability of the gospels may wish to consult Blomberg (1987), and for John's gospel in particular, Blomberg (2001). On the Gospels as eyewitness testimony, see Bauckham (2017), and for a contemporary assessment of Lewis's arguments in "Modern Theology and Biblical Criticism" in *Christian Reflections*, see Bauckham (2013: 152–66). Rainbow (2014: 148–72) provides an overview of pertinent passages concerning the deity of Christ in John's Gospel; Just (2018) surveys the forty-five times Jesus uses the expression "I am" or is quoted as doing so in John's gospel. On the significance of Jesus's forgiveness of sins, Davis provides a helpful discussion of Mark 2:1–12 (2009: 39–48). Brazier looks at the place of the trilemma in the history of theology (2012: 103–26).

5 Mere Christianity

5.1 Mere Freedom

In *Broadcast Talks* and *Beyond Personality*, two of the three books that became the basis for *Mere Christianity*, Lewis emphasized the role of free will in coming to faith and continuing in that faith. Except for changing a single contraction, he used the very same wording in *Mere Christianity:*

> [A] Christian can lose the Christ-life which has been put into him, and has to make efforts to keep it. (Lewis 1942: 59; Lewis 2001b: 62–63)

> He says, "if you let me, I will make you perfect . . . You have free will, and if you choose, you can push Me away." (Lewis 1944: 45; Lewis 2001b: 202)

> What He is watching and waiting and working for is something that is not easy even for God, because, from the nature of the case, even He cannot produce it by a mere act of power. He is waiting and watching for it both in Miss Bates and in Dick Firkin. It is something they can freely give Him or

freely refuse to Him. Will they, or will they not, turn to Him and thus fulfil the only purpose for which they were created? (Lewis 1944: 52; Lewis 2001b: 211–12)

[Y]ou must realise from the outset that the goal towards which He is beginning to guide you is absolute perfection; and no power in the whole universe, *except you yourself* [emphasis added], can prevent Him from taking you to that goal. (Lewis 1944: 46; Lewis 2001b: 202)

The world does not consist of 100 per cent. Christians and 100 per cent. non-Christians. There are people (a great many of them) who are slowly ceasing to be Christians but who still call themselves by that name: some of them are clergymen. (Lewis 1944: 50; Lewis 2001b: 208)

As is apparent from the passages above, on this view of freedom, what Miss Bates and Dick Firkin do is up to them; they have the power to accept God and the power to reject Him. Burson and Walls highlight the implications of this:

Lewis is affirming libertarian freedom. It is worth noting that in *Mere Christianity*, a book dedicated to the common core beliefs of all Christians, Lewis includes a vision of human liberty that entails the power of contrary choice. (Burson and Walls 1998: 75)

Such power is incompatible with "antecedent conditions and/or causal laws" determining a person's choice (Plantinga 1977: 29), where determining antecedent conditions includes divine actions. "Will they, or will they not, turn to Him?" is incompatible with Calvinist affirmations of irresistible grace, and "There are people . . . who are slowly ceasing to be Christians" is at odds with the Calvinist commitment to the perseverance of the saints. It seems, then, that Lewis would have regarded Calvinists, who take these doctrines to be soteriological essentials, to have erred in their understanding. That is, unless Lewis had second thoughts about free choice.

There are passages in Lewis's subsequent writings that seem to suggest a shift in his perspective. When commenting on his own conversion in an interview toward the end of his life, Lewis appeared to downplay the significance of his choice:

Mr Wirt: Do you feel that you made a decision at the time of your conversion?
Lewis: I would not put it that way. . . . I feel my decision was not so important. I was the object rather than the subject in this affair. I was decided upon. . . . at the moment what I heard was God saying, "Put down your gun and we'll talk."
Mr Wirt: That sounds to me as if you came to a very definite point of decision.

Lewis: Well, I would say that the most deeply compelled action is also the freest action. By that I mean no part of you is outside the action. It is a paradox. (Lewis 1970: 261)

Along with this autobiographical reflection, there are passages in Lewis's correspondence with Mrs Mary Van Deusen, October 20, 1952 (Lewis 2007: 237–38), and Mrs Emily McLay, August 3, 1953 (354–55), where he appears to back off from any definite view regarding free will and divine sovereignty:

> All that Calvinist question – Free-Will & Predestination, is to my mind undiscussable, insoluble.... When we carry it [Freedom and Necessity] up to relations between God & Man, has the distinction perhaps become non-sensical? After all, when we are most free, it is only with a freedom God has given us: and when our will is most influenced by Grace, it is still *our will*. And if what *our will* does is not "voluntary," and if "voluntary" does not mean "free," what are we talking about? I'd leave it all alone. (237–38)

> What I *think* is this. Everyone looking back on *his own* conversion must feel – and I am sure the feeling is in some sense true – "It is not *I* who have done this. I did not choose Christ: He chose me" ... It then seems to us logical & natural to turn this personal experience into a general rule "All conversions depend on God's choice." But this I believe is exactly what we must not do: for generalisations are legitimate only when we are dealing with matters to which our faculties are adequate. (354–55)

Lewis's remarks to Mrs Van Deusen and Mrs McLay are puzzling because he wrote them not long after publishing *Mere Christianity* (July 7, 1952). "Leave it alone" and talk of inadequate faculties clash with earlier quotations on free will. It is implausible to suppose that when Lewis wrote to Mrs. Van Deusen, he had abandoned the views on free will that he had already published in *Broadcast Talks* (1942) and *Beyond Personality* (1944), and just incorporated into *Mere Christianity*.

Lewis's responses to Mr Wirt on May 7, 1963 (date found in Duriez 2005: 292) are also puzzling. Lewis's revision of *Miracles* came out in 1960, and in it he repeated verbatim what he had written in the original 1947 version of *Miracles* where he underscored divine surrender:

> The sin, both of men and of angels, was rendered possible by the fact that God gave them free will: thus surrendering a portion of His omnipotence ... because He saw that from a world of free creatures, even though they fell, He could work out ... a deeper happiness and a fuller splendour than any world of automata would admit. (Lewis 2001c: 196–97 [reprint of 1960]; 1947: 147)

It would be odd if Lewis abandoned his long-standing view of God "surrendering a portion of omnipotence," but it is also hard to see how it could fit in with "I was the object rather than the subject of the affair. I was decided upon" (Lewis 1979: 261).

Is there a way to reconcile Lewis's comments to Mrs Van Deusen and Mrs McLay, and his remarks about his conversion with the affirmations of free will in *Mere Christianity* and in *Miracles?* Scott R. Burson and Jerry L. Walls provide a plausible perspective:

> When Lewis discusses this subject in the more rigorous philosophical realm he offers a vision of freedom and predestination that is self-consistent and coherent. But when he attempts to translate this subject into the domain of the colloquial and concrete, his clarity clouds. One can certainly understand why, for how could we ever solve this issue in the realm of the particular? We cannot know the precise interrelationship between divine and human causation, nor can we trace a specific action to any particular motive or cause. How could we? Lewis is correct in saying that such a pursuit is pointless. (1998: 104)

A letter Lewis wrote to Mr. Beimer on September 7, 1962 (2007: 1356–57) illustrates the distinction Burson and Walls make between the philosophical and the "colloquial and the concrete." In this late letter – in contrast to the ones written to Mrs. Van Deusen on October 20, 1952, and Mrs. Mclay on August 3, 1953 – Lewis was working in "the more rigorous philosophical realm" and gave a "self–consistent and coherent" argument for free will:

> Therefore *either* there is no reason to suppose that human thinking is of any value at all and therefore no reason to believe in CE [Cause-and-Effect nexus] or in anything else: *or* the particular chains of events we call "logical thinking" are sufficiently free from the CE nexus to be determined by the quite different GC [Ground and Consequent] nexus.
>
> But, if so, it must equally be possible that the particular events we call moral choices can be sufficiently free from the CE nexus to be determined by some different kind of nexus – i.e. to be *self-determined*. Hence the absolutely universal conviction that we are free to choose need not be an illusion. And since it is implied in all our moral judgements . . . it is reasonable to accept the universal conviction. (2007: 1356–57)

If Burson and Walls' comments regarding the context of Lewis's assertions about free will are correct, then Lewis never abandoned his belief in libertarian freedom, the sort of freedom he expressed as an essential aspect of the faith in *Mere Christianity.*

For Further Reading: Adam Barkman argues that theological differences between Lewis and Calvinists "are not, or do not have to be, as large as Lewis and many Calvinists think" (2011: 26).

5.2 God, Freedom, and Evil

Christianity presupposes the presence of evil, for the Christian message of forgiveness assumes that God's moral law has been broken. At the same time Christianity teaches that God is perfectly powerful and good, and those perfections appear to be incompatible with the presence of evil. C.S. Lewis sums up the problem of evil:

> If God were good, He would wish to make His creatures perfectly happy, and if God were almighty He would be able to do what He wished. But the creatures are not happy. Therefore God lacks either goodness, or power, or both. (Lewis 2001d: 16)

The reasoning in Lewis's summation is valid, an instance of modus tollens: If P then Q, not Q, so not P.

> If P: *God were perfectly good and powerful*, then Q: *God's creatures would be happy.*
> Not Q: *God's creatures are not happy.*
> Therefore, Not P: *It is false that God is perfectly good and powerful.*

Given the validity of the reasoning, the argument's success depends upon how its key concepts – perfect power, and perfect goodness and happiness – are understood. If perfect power meant that with God, 1) absolutely nothing is impossible, 2) perfect goodness required providing every rational creature (hereafter creature) with a self-satisfying, contented, pain-free existence, and 3) that perfect happiness called for self-satisfied, contented, pain-free lives all around, then the argument would indeed show that the existence of evil is incompatible with God's existence. Lewis, however, would have none of that.

Lewis held that if God is all-powerful, then God can do whatever is intrinsically possible, whatever is free of contradiction. God can create unicorns, red barns, and entire worlds, but not two-horned unicorns, colorless red barns, and uncreated worlds, "meaningless combinations of words do not suddenly acquire meaning simply because we prefix to them 'God can.'" (18).

If God is all-good as well as all-powerful, God can make covenants and protect the innocent. He cannot break covenants or torture the innocent. Those actions, like creating an uncreated world, are contradictory. To see why, it is helpful to consider a Socratic question Lewis knew well. In Plato's dialogue, *The Euthyphro,* Socrates asks, "Is what is holy holy because the gods approve it, or do they approve it because it is holy?" (Plato 1961: 178). Translated into a monotheistic context, we could have something like: "Are these things [moral laws] right because God commands them or does God command them because they are right?" (Lewis 1967a: 79). If the theist takes God's commands to be the sole basis of rightness, then the theist is saddled with moral absurdities. God could have made rape and murder right actions, and the commandment "Thou shalt commit adultery," in the so-called Wicked Bible (McGrath 2002: 216), need not have been a misprint. On the other hand, if theists hold that God commands the moral law because it is right, then the moral law would appear to be independent of God, and we would be "compelled to think of Him, making it in conformity with some yet more ultimate pattern of goodness (in which case that pattern, and not He, would be supreme)" (Lewis 1967a: 80).

In "The Poison of Subjectivism" Lewis pointed to a third possibility. "But it might be permissible to lay down two negations: that God neither *obeys* nor *creates* the moral law. . . . God is not merely good, but goodness; goodness is not merely divine, but God" (80). If God is by His very nature good, "Good Himself" (Lewis 2001d: 159), then God could no more break a promise or torture the innocent than an iron anvil could float. With God, wrong actions are intrinsic impossibilities.

Unlike scourging the guiltless, there is nothing inconsistent about a perfectly good and powerful God creating free rational creatures with the ability to make morally significant choices. However, not even an all-powerful God could make them freely choose to act rightly. "Christianity asserts that God is good; that He made all things good . . . that one of the good things He made, namely, the free will of rational creatures, by its very nature included the possibility of evil" (63). As indicated in "Mere Freedom" above, Lewis considered genuine freedom to be libertarian freedom and therefore incompatible with divine determinism. So, determining a creaturely free choice is an intrinsic impossibility and therefore outside of God's power. Creatures free to act rightly are free to act wrongly.

In elaborating the conditions needed for creatures to choose, Lewis issued a caution, "What follows is to be regarded as less an assertion of what they are than a sample of what they might be" (19). Lewis thought a common environment with "a fixed nature of its own" (22) might be necessary. That stability would enable creatures to interact and accommodate morally significant choices. Fire can be used to cook a neighbor's dinner or burn her house down. God could, on occasion, put out house fires, but constant intervention is not possible in a world where creatures have free will. "[A] world in which God corrected . . . so that a wooden beam became soft as grass when it was used as a weapon. . . . would be one in which wrong actions were impossible, and in which, therefore, freedom of the will would be void" (24).

The basic choice of every creature is loving God more than the self, or the self more than God. Its proper good "is to surrender itself to its Creator – to enact intellectually, volitionally, and emotionally, that relationship which is given in the mere fact of its being a creature" (88). Obeying and submitting to God, as befits the creature-Creator relationship leads to fulfillment. Disobeying and rebelling against God, which is contrary to the appropriate creature-Creator relationship, results in frustration. Lewis refers to the decision of "choosing God or self for the centre," as "the terrible alternative" (70). Terrible because the consequences are so momentous. Each creature faces the prospect of "utter satisfaction" or ruin:

> All that you are, sins apart, is destined, if you will let God have His good way, to utter satisfaction. (152)

> To be a complete man means to have the passions obedient to the will and the will offered to God: to *have been* a man – to be an ex-man or "damned ghost" – would presumably mean to consist of a will utterly centered in its self and passions utterly uncontrolled by the will. (128)

A perfectly good God would want every creature to be completely satisfied and would attempt to prevent any creature's ruin. And so God does. Piling analogy on analogy, Lewis describes God's love as "persistent as the artist's love for his work and despotic as a man's love for his dog, provident and venerable as a father's love for a child, jealous, inexorable, exacting as love between the sexes" (39). For creatures who have not surrendered to their Creator in obedience and submission, "Goodness itself" uses pain as a corrective. It is impossible to ignore and shatters the illusion of self-sufficiency. A rebel forced to recognize that its independence is an impossibility may choose to change its center from self to God. May, but need not: "In creating beings with free will, omnipotence from the outset submits to the possibility of such defeat" (129).

Returning to the initial objection:

> "If God were good, He would wish to make His creatures perfectly happy, and if God were almighty He would be able to do what He wished. But the creatures are not happy. Therefore, God lacks either goodness, or power, or both." (16)

God is indeed good and does wish to make His creatures perfectly happy, utterly satisfied. Creatures have free will and so not even omnipotence can make them freely choose to love God more than self. If they do not, they will not be happy, but they will have chosen their misery. "To be God – to be like God and to share His goodness in creaturely response – to be miserable – these are the only three alternatives" (47).

For Further Reading: Philip Tallon (2015) notes that Lewis's approach to the problem of evil anticipated Alvin Plantinga's free will defense and John Hick's soul-making theodicy. Michael Peterson (2017) explores how Lewis would respond to the evidential argument from gratuitous evil. Jerry Root (2009) examines the connection between subjectivism and evil in a variety of Lewis's writings. Colin Duriez (2015a) considers the battle between good and evil – in the seen and unseen realms – in the writings of C.S. Lewis and J.R.R. Tolkien.

5.3 Trinity and Incarnation

When N.T. Wright was a College Chaplain and a student said, "I don't believe in god," he gave a stock response: "Oh, that's interesting; which god is it you don't believe in?" (Wright 1998). After the student had given a "spy-in-the-sky" description Wright would reply, "Well, I'm not surprised you don't believe in that god. I don't believe in that god either" (Wright 1998).

If a student had asked C.S. Lewis, *What do you mean by God?* C.S. Lewis would have replied, "Love Himself" (1960b: 11) and noted that "Love is something that one person has for another person" (2001b: 174). And as a "mere Christian" who affirmed the doctrine of the Trinity, he might well have been sympathetic to Richard Swinburne's argument that a loving God requires at least three persons.

> Love involves sharing, giving to the other what of one's own is good for him and receiving from the other what of his is good for one; and love involves co-operating with another to benefit third parties. . . . There would be something deeply unsatisfying . . . about a marriage in which the parties were concerned solely with each other and did not use their mutual love to bring forth good to others . . . Love must share and love must co-operate in sharing. (Swinburne 1994: 177–78)

As one cube contains six squares, so God is "a being who is three Persons while remaining one Being" (Lewis 2001b: 162). In explaining the relationship between the first two persons, Lewis borrowed a distinction from the Nicene Creed, "begotten, not made."

> To beget is to become the father of: to create is to make. . . . When you beget, you beget something of the same kind as yourself. A man begets human babies, a beaver begets little beavers . . . But when you make, you make something of a different kind from yourself. A bird makes a nest, a beaver builds a dam. (157)

As the first person of the Trinity begets the second, we refer to them as "God the Father" and "God the Son." What is unique about this begetting is that there is no temporal sequence, "there never was a time before the Father produced the Son" (173). After attempting to convey the difficult notion of nontemporal begetting, Lewis noted that "the most important thing to know is that it [the Father-Son relation] is "a relation of love" (174). The third person of the Trinity comes from this relation: "What grows out of the joint life of the Father and Son is a real Person, is in fact the Third of the three Persons who are God" (175).

God's existence as three loving persons squares well with the standard theistic belief that God had no need to create. Brian Hebblethwaite comments:

> If personal analogies are held to yield some insight into the divine nature . . . then there can be no doubt that the model of a single individual person does create difficulties for theistic belief. It presents us with a picture of one who . . . is unable to enjoy the excellence of personal relation unless he first create an object for his love. Monotheistic faiths have not favored the idea that creation is necessary to God, but short of postulating personal relation in God, it is difficult to see how they can avoid it. (1987: 14)

God freely and graciously chose to create and – when His creatures freely and ungratefully rebelled – God met ingratitude with graciousness. God the Son humbled Himself, taking on the form of a servant (Phil 2:5–7). It was as if a playwright became one of the actors.

> Shakespeare could, in principle, make himself appear as Author within the play, and write a dialogue between Hamlet and himself. The "Shakespeare" within the play would of course be at once Shakespeare and one of Shakespeare's creatures. It would bear some analogy to Incarnation. (Lewis 1955b: 227)

The Incarnate Son of God is fully human and fully divine:

> The doctrine that our Lord was God and man . . . means that a real man (human body *and* human soul) was in Him so united with the 2nd Person of the Trinity as to make one Person: just as in you and me a complete anthropoid animal (animal body *and* animal "soul" i.e. instincts, sensations etc) is so united with an immortal rational soul as to be one person. (Lewis 2004b: 764)

Determining what it means to be fully human requires distinguishing between common human properties and essential ones:

> A common human property will be one which many or most human beings have. . . . We need to be clear that a property's being common or even universal for members of a kind does not entail that it is essential for the kind . . . the property of living at some time on the surface of the earth is a common human property . . . it is not essential for being human. (Morris 1986: 63)

To be fully human is to possess all essential human properties, and for Lewis, that included the possibility of a mistaken belief.

Reflecting on Mark 13:30, Lewis referred to Jesus's remark, "Truly, I say to you, this generation will not pass away until all these things take place" as "certainly the most embarrassing verse in the Bible" (Lewis 2017: 98). Embarrassing, for as Lewis read Mark chapter 13, "these things" included Jesus's return:

> It is certainly the most embarrassing verse in the Bible. Yet how teasing, also, that within fourteen words of it should come the statement "But of that day and that hour knoweth no man, no, not the angels which are in heaven, neither the Son, but the Father." The one exhibition of error and the one a confession of ignorance grow side by side. That they stood thus in the mouth of Jesus himself, and were not merely placed thus by the reporter, we surely need not doubt. Unless the reporter were perfectly honest he would never have recorded the confession of ignorance at all.... The facts, then, are these: that Jesus professed Himself (in some sense) ignorant, and within a moment showed that He really was so. (105)

That Jesus confessed ignorance is – given the reliability of the gospel account – indisputable. That Jesus's claim about "this generation" is false is another matter. Though Lewis did not mention it, Jesus followed that claim with a remarkable assertion about the weightiness of his words: "Heaven and earth will pass away, but my words will not pass away" (Mark 13:31 ESV). If Lewis's reading is correct, this verse adds to the embarrassment, calling into question the general reliability of Jesus's teachings. Whether or not God Incarnate could have made a false theological claim is not a matter to explore, much less settle here. By itself, Mark 13:31 suggests that Jesus would not have thought so. For now, perhaps it will be enough to show that on the reading of one preeminent New Testament scholar, N.T. Wright, there is nothing to be embarrassed about.

Wright makes four fundamental points: First, Mark 13 is about the fall of the Jerusalem temple (Wright 2001: 178). Next, in this context, talk of Jesus's return would be a category mistake:

> We must, however, stress again: as far as the disciples, good first-century Jews as they were, were concerned, there was no reason whatever for them to be thinking about the end of the space-time universe.... They had not yet even thought of his [Jesus] being taken from them, let alone that he might come back. (1996: 345)

Further, if Jesus had been talking about a literal end of the space-time world, He would not have counseled His disciples to flee: "Had it been the end of the world, what would have been the point of running away so frantically?" (2001: 183). Finally, it is essential to note that Jesus's words, "they will see the Son of Man coming in clouds with great power and glory" (Mark 13: 26), are an allusion to Daniel 7, and there the topic is the Son of Man's return to the Ancient of Days, not His descent from the heavens.

Daniel 7 conceives the scene from the perspective of heaven, not earth. The "son of man" figure "comes" to the Ancient of Days. He comes *from* earth *to* heaven (1996: 361).

> I saw in the night visions,
>   and behold, with the clouds of heaven
>   there came one like a son of man
> and he came to the Ancient of Days
>   and was presented before him.
>   *(Daniel 7:13 ESV)*

Pace Lewis, Jesus did not claim in Mark 13 that he would return within a generation. So then, even if Lewis were right to think that making false claims is compatible with being fully human and fully divine, at least on N.T. Wright's reading, Mark 13 is not the place to make that case.

Mere Christians may differ as to what they believe constitutes full humanity and divinity. However, they should agree that becoming human was not simply a passing phase in the life of God the Son:

> It seems to me that I seldom meet any strong or exultant sense of the continued, never-to-be-abandoned, Humanity of Christ in glory, in eternity. We stress the Humanity too exclusively at Christmas, and the Deity too exclusively after the Resurrection; almost as if Christ once became a man and then presently reverted to being simply God. We think of the Resurrection and Ascension (rightly) as great acts of God; less often as the triumph of Man. (Lewis 1986b: 134)

For Further Reading: Favorite readings of Lewis include Athanasius, *On the Incarnation of the Word* (1946) and Dorothy L. Sayers' *The Man Born to be King* (1943), which Lewis read every year during Holy Week since its publication (Lewis 1982: 93). For more information on the Augustinian background of C.S. Lewis's account of the Trinity, see Ross (2012).

5.4 The Central Christian Belief/Atonement

Among the beliefs that make up "mere Christianity" one stands out: "The central Christian belief is that Christ's death has somehow put us right with God and given us a fresh start" (Lewis 2001b: 54). Lewis stated that before he became a Christian he thought that he needed to affirm one particular theory about this belief which he summed up – some would say caricatured (Rigney 2018: 60) – as follows: "God wanted to punish men for having deserted and joined the Great Rebel, but Christ volunteered to be punished instead, and God let us off" (Lewis 2001b: 53). Though

Lewis did not name the theory, he had in mind penal substitutionary atonement. He dismissed it as implausible, "immoral," and "silly" (54).

In contrast to penal substitutionary atonement, Lewis mentioned his own theory. On that account, God the Son Incarnate also plays a substitutionary role, but that role is not one of punishment but repentance, "willing submission to humiliation and a kind of death" (57):

> [W]e now need God's help in order to do something which God, in His own nature, never does at all – to surrender, to suffer, to submit, to die. . . . But supposing God became a man – suppose our human nature which can suffer and die was amalgamated with God's nature in one person – then that person could help us. He could surrender His will, and suffer and die, because He was man; and He could do it perfectly because He was God. (57–58)

Despite the stark contrast between the two substitutionary theories, in one sense Lewis considered them on equal footing; neither one is an essential component of "mere Christianity." And of his own view, Lewis wrote, "Do not mistake it for the thing itself; and if it does not help you, drop it" (59).

What is essential to "mere Christianity" is what Christ accomplished:

> We are told that Christ was killed for us, that His death has washed out our sins, and that by dying He disabled death itself. That is the formula. That is Christianity. (55)

> You can say that Christ died for our sins. You may say that the Father has forgiven us because Christ has done for us what we ought to have done. You may say that we are washed in the blood of the Lamb. You may say that Christ has defeated death. They are all true. If any of them do not appeal to you, leave it alone and get on with the formula that does. (181–82)

Since all the formulas come from the Bible, it is odd to find Lewis telling his readers to drop what doesn't appeal to them. It would make sense though, if the readers Lewis had in mind were non-Christians. In that case his advice would be, *Don't put off becoming a Christian because you do not understand or cannot relate to one of the metaphors the Bible uses to describe Christ's work*, and would be of a piece with his counsel to avoid letting a theory about how the atonement works become a stumbling block.

That Lewis had non-Christians in mind in the above passage becomes clear from Lewis's imaginary correspondence between two believers, *Letters to Malcolm Chiefly on Prayer*. There the advice is neither to drop what does not appeal, nor to replace biblical images with one's own:

> If we are free to delete all inconvenient data we shall certainly have no theological difficulties; but for the same reason no solutions and no

progress.... The troublesome fact, the apparent absurdity which can't be fitted in to any synthesis we have yet made, is precisely the one we must not ignore. (1964: 59)

Trying to get in behind the [biblical] analogy, you go further and fare worse. You suggest that what is traditionally regarded as our experience of God's anger would be more helpfully regarded as what inevitably happens to us if we behave inappropriately towards a reality of immense power.... My dear Malcolm, what do you suppose you have gained by substituting the image of a live wire for that of angered majesty? You have shut us all up in despair; for the angry can forgive, and electricity can't. (96)

Lewis made it clear in a letter to Mr. Young that settling on a single biblical image would be a mistake:

I think the ideas of sacrifice, Ransom, Championship (over Death), Substitution, etc. are all images to *suggest* the reality (not otherwise comprehensible to us) of the Atonement. To fix on any *one* of them as if it contained and limited the truth like a scientific definition wd. in my opinion be a mistake. (2007: 1476)

And in his portrayal of Aslan's death Lewis avoided that error:

Lewis's incorporation ... of such a wide range of theologians is most extraordinary. He accomplishes the feat, logically enough, by interweaving *substitutionary* language (Aslan's blood is shed, the lion is Edmund's substitute, the deeper magic is invoked by the Emperor-over-the-Sea) with *ransom* imagery (the Witch has rights over traitors, is "tricked" by the deeper magic, and Aslan is Edmund's ransom) and glowing *subjective* incentive to emulate the majestic Aslan. (Vanderhorst 2009)

For Further Reading: Anderson (2016/17) presents Lewis's rejection of penal substitutionary atonement as "A Problem Case for New Calvinist Theology." Rigney (2018: 59–67) critiques Lewis's dismissal of penal substitution. Taliaferro (2022) surveys the atonement theme in The Chronicles of Narnia, defends a Christus Victor Ransom theory, and shows how that theory complements classic and contemporary atonement theories. Adam J. Johnson (2022) turns to Lewis's Ransom trilogy to consider "the cosmological implications of the Christus Victor theory."

6 The Christian Life

6.1 Faith

C.S. Lewis's second novel in the Ransom Trilogy, *Perelandra*, begins with the narrator – call him Clive – recounting a walk from a train station to his friend

Elwin Ransom's cottage. As Clive approached Ransom's home, his emotions and imagination began to take hold of him. He felt that he was on the verge of a nervous breakdown and imagined that Ransom had either been duped by, or was in league with, malevolent supernatural creatures. His reason, however, told him something different: "The reader, not knowing Ransom, will not understand how contrary to all reason this *idea* [emphasis added] was. The rational part of my mind, even at the very moment, knew perfectly well that even if the whole universe was hostile, Ransom was sane and wholesome and honest" (1965b: 13). Clive followed his reason over and against his emotions and imagination, continuing to believe that Ransom was trustworthy, and completed his journey to Ransom's cottage. In C.S. Lewis's terminology, Clive exercised faith: "Now Faith, in the sense in which I am using the word, is the art of holding on to things your reason has once accepted, in spite of your changing moods" (2001b: 140).

This kind of faith, call it belief-that faith, is concerned with propositions. There is nothing inherently Christian about it. Without it "you can never be either a sound Christian or a sound atheist, but just a creature dithering to and fro, with its beliefs really dependent on the weather and the state of its digestion" (141).

> When one has developed the habit of holding on to beliefs, accepted on the basis of reason – moods be blasted – one has the virtue of faith. In order to develop that virtue one must regularly attend to one's beliefs. In the case of a Christian, that includes daily prayers, reflection on doctrine and participation in the life of church, for beliefs "must be fed." (141)

Lewis contrasted belief-that faith with a higher faith, call it belief-in faith or trust. Here, the object of faith is not a proposition but a person, the person of Christ. This faith arises out of crisis. When one has tried one's hardest to practice Christianity, repeatedly failed, and recognized one's utter inadequacy, the stage is set for unqualified trust in God the Son:

> The sense in which a Christian leaves it to God is that he puts all his trust in Christ: trusts that Christ will somehow share with him the perfect obedience which He carried out from His birth to His crucifixion: that Christ will make the man more like himself and, in a sense, make good his deficiencies. (147)

When one moves from belief-that to belief-in, one shifts from "the logic of speculative thought" to "the logic of personal relations" (Lewis 2017: 30). In *The Lion, the Witch, and the Wardrobe*, one of The Chronicles of Narnia, Lucy, the youngest of four siblings, is adamant about having visited another world, "I don't care what you think or what you say . . . I know I've met a Faun in there" (2000a: 46). Her older siblings, Peter and Susan, assume that she is mistaken.

When they share that assumption with their host Professor Kirk, they are surprised by his response. He says, regarding the falseness of Lucy's claims, "That is more than I know ... and a charge against someone you have always found truthful is a very serious thing; a very serious thing indeed" (48). Were Peter and Susan to consider claims about the existence of Fauns – in a purely theoretical sense – they might think evidence for them is lacking. If it turned out that they were wrong, their mistake would have been about the truth value of a statement, "Fauns exist." Were they to consider claims about the existence of Fauns – in light of their sister's testimony – and reach the same conclusion, their mistake would have been about the honesty and/or sanity of their sister, "a very serious thing indeed." If Peter and Susan had very strong evidence for Lucy's reliability, it might well have been appropriate for them to accept her otherwise astounding claim.

The distinction between the logic of speculative thought, and the logic of personal relations, takes on immeasurably more importance when the relation is between a Christian and God. Lewis supposed that if one believed the central claims of the Christian worldview, one would do so only after evaluating the evidence for them. Among the claims that comprise the Christian worldview are: God is infinitely wiser and more benevolent than any Christian, and the Christian's trust in God will be tested. Assuming that one affirmed the Christian worldview on the basis of good evidence one would be justified in continuing to trust in the face of contrary evidence, for "the content of our original belief by logical necessity entails the proposition that such behaviour is appropriate" (Lewis 2017: 24). Failure to trust Christ once the shift has been made from the logic of speculative thought to the logic of personal relations, is not a theoretical error but a failure to love, for "To love involves trusting the beloved beyond the evidence, even against the evidence" (252–56).

For further reading: On the question, Did C.S. Lewis lose his faith?, see (Beversluis 2007: 303–11) and (Purtill 2006: 227–52).

6.2 Prayer

Nine-year-old Jack Lewis prayed for his mother's healing from cancer. She died. Looking back, the adult Lewis offered these reflections on this episode:

> When her case was pronounced hopeless I remembered what I had been taught; that prayers offered in faith would be granted. I accordingly set myself to produce by will power a firm belief that my prayers for her recovery would be successful; and, as I thought, I achieved it. When nevertheless she died I shifted my ground and worked myself into a belief that there was to be a miracle. . . . The thing hadn't worked, but I was used to things not working, and I thought no more about it. . . . I had approached God, or my idea of God,

without love, without awe, even without fear. He was, in my mental
picture ... a magician; and when He had done what was required of Him
I supposed He would simply – well, go away. (1955b: 20–21)

In *A Grief Observed*, where Lewis shared his anguish over another death to
cancer and another case of unanswered prayer, he exclaimed, "Not my idea of
God, but God" (2001a: 67) and referred to God as "the great iconoclast" (66). In
his final work *Letters to Malcolm Chiefly on Prayer*, Lewis wrote that "The
prayer preceding all prayers is 'May it be the real I that speaks. May it be the real
Thou that I speak to'" (1964: 82).

At the center of prayer is the relationship between creature and creator:

(Prayer in the sense of petition, asking for things, is a small part of it;
confession and penitence are its threshold, adoration its sanctuary, the presence and vision and enjoyment of God its bread and wine.) In it God shows
Himself to us. (2017: 7)

Though petition may only be a small part of prayer, there is no license to overlook
it, as it is an essential feature of The Lord's Prayer: "Give us this day our daily
bread." As a child, Lewis had been taught "that prayers offered in faith would be
granted" (1955b: 20). As an adult, Lewis reflected on those teachings. In
"Petitionary Prayer: A Problem Without an Answer," Lewis contrasted
"*A* Pattern prayers," conditional prayers: "Thy will be done" (1967a:143), with
"*B* Pattern prayers," requiring "faith that the particular thing the petitioner asks
will be given him" (144). Together they demanded of the petitioner an untenable
frame of mind: "How is it possible to say, simultaneously, 'I firmly believe that
Thou wilt give me this,' *and*, 'If Thou shalt deny me it, Thy will be done'? How
can one mental act both exclude possible refusal and consider it?" (2007: 281).

Unable to solve the theoretical conundrum, Lewis arrived at a practical solution.
The prayers of unwavering faith are for "very advanced pupils" (1964: 60). As
Lewis did not count himself in that class, he had no need to worry about a conflict
between unwavering and conditional prayers. Further, if he had ever been able to
pray with unwavering faith, it would have been clear that it was God's will that he
do so, ruling out any conflict with the conditional form of prayer.

Lewis believed one kind of petitionary prayer to be outside of God's will. In
a chapter on "cursings" in *Reflections on the Psalms*, he referred to imprecatory
prayers as "devilish" (1986b: 20), "diabolical," and "hideously distorted by the
human instrument" (32), and cited Psalm 109 as an example:

Appoint a wicked man against him;
    let an accuser stand at his right hand.
May his days be few;
    may another take his office!

> May his children be fatherless
>   and his wife a widow!
> May his children wander around and beg. (Psalm 109:7-10a, ESV)

Though Lewis considered these curses to be morally repugnant, he found some spiritual value in them. They can be an occasion for addressing our own resentments and reflecting on the consequences that can come from harming others (1986b: 23–24).

Lewis did well to address curses in the psalms, "Where we find a difficulty we may always expect that a discovery awaits us" (28). But he did not go nearly far enough. Elizabeth Anscombe noted that in rejecting some passages, Lewis overlooked their presence in the New Testament:

> Mr. Lewis, for example, thus condemns a passage in the psalms: "Let their table be made a snare to take themselves withal" which is quoted *con amore* by St. Paul, who applies it to the unbelieving among the Jews (Romans XI, 9). This, according to Mr. Lewis, is a "refinement of malice." He equally condemns attitudes faithfully reproduced in the Apocalypse. (Anscombe 2019: 177)

In a similar vein, one might mention Peter's appeal in Acts 1:20 to two of the psalms Lewis found problematic: 69 and 109.

Far removed from imprecations are the Psalms' expressions of adoration. At one time Lewis found admonitions to praise God problematic; he could not grasp "this perpetual eulogy" (Lewis 1986b: 91). Demands to praise recalled insecure people seeking reassurance and toadies applauding dictators (90). He changed his mind when he realized that failure to admire, say, a beautiful painting would reveal our inadequacies. Admiration may be the appropriate response to a painting, and "if we do not admire we shall be stupid, insensible, and great losers" (92). But then, all the more so with God: "He is that Object to admire which . . . is simply to be awake, to have entered the real world; not to appreciate which is to have lost the greatest experience, and in the end to have lost all" (92). If a creature were able to fully delight in God, and give his delight perfect expression, the creature would be "in supreme beatitude" (96).

For Further Reading: James M. Houston (1989) describes six traits of Lewis's prayer life. Donald T. Williams (2007) introduces, summarizes, and analyzes Lewis's *Reflections on the Psalms*. Charles Taliaferro's devotional work enables the reader to pray "in the way that Lewis did about issues and themes that were central to his experience" (1998: 8).

6.3 Theosis / The Weight of Glory

On June 8, 1941, C.S. Lewis preached "The Weight of Glory" in the twelfth century Oxford University Church of St. Mary the Virgin. Walter Hooper described it as "so magnificent" as to be "worthy of a place with some of the Church Fathers" (Lewis 1980: xxi). In *The C.S. Lewis Readers' Encyclopedia*, Marvin Hinton's final words were "A masterpiece" (1998: 423). At the end of his sermon, Lewis contrasted corruption with deification:

> It is a serious thing to live in a society of possible gods and goddesses, to remember that the dullest and most uninteresting person you can talk to may one day be a creature which, if you say [sic] it now, you would be strongly tempted to worship, or else a horror and a corruption such as you meet, if at all, only in a nightmare. (2001a: 18–19)

This language was not hyperbole for the pulpit. Similar phrases appear throughout Lewis's writings: "He will make the feeblest and filthiest of us into a god or goddess" (2001b: 205–6); "the Divine Life ... calls us to be gods" (1970: 112); "We shall be true and everlasting divine persons only in Heaven" (1980: 119); "when we shall be those gods that we are described as being in Scripture" (Psalm 82:6; John 10:34–36; Lewis 1970: 87); "Now get on with it. Become a god" (Lewis 2001a: 72).

Athanasius wrote in *On the Incarnation*, "He [God the Son], indeed, assumed humanity that we might become God" (1946: 86). Christopher Armstrong reflects on the significance of this work for Lewis:

> Lewis had first read his Greek edition of Athanasius's *De Incarnatione* on Christmas Eve 1942 (years prior to writing the introduction to his friend Sister Penelope's translation). The holy day of this and a subsequent reading (Good Friday 1958) indicate that he read the book not only with a scholarly interest but also devotionally. (2016: 197)

Lewis's view on the purpose of the incarnation, "The Son of God became a man to enable men to become sons of God" (2001b: 178), was in line with the views of Athanasius and Eastern Christianity:

> [I]n the understanding of the Christian East salvation involves nothing less than *theosis*, "deification" or "divinisation." We humans are called to be "partakers of the divine nature" (2 Peter 1:4), to share by grace – in a direct and unmediated manner – in the transforming life and glory of God. Such is likewise Lewis's understanding of salvation: "Century by century God has guided nature up to the point of producing creatures which can (if they will) be taken right out of nature, turned into 'gods.'" Lewis would have come across the idea of *theosis* in the work of St. Athanasius, *The Incarnation of the Word of God*. (Ware 1998: 67)

Note that conceptual agreement does not necessitate identical vocabulary:

> Avoiding the technical language of theology, Lewis anticipates our glorious future in glowing figures of speech which convey the meaning of *theosis* better than the word itself. (Beyer 2006: 90)

Nor does agreement require acquaintance with the same source materials. Dom Bede Griffins notes that "Lewis showed very little interest in the Fathers of the Church" (Griffiths 2005: 89–90). Where Lewis "reached conclusions Eastern Christians could wholeheartedly endorse" he did so "starting from Western premises" (Ware 1998: 55).

Ralph C. Wood notes the distinction between "image" and "likeness" in the Eastern Orthodox Church, and Chris Jensen comments on its soteriological significance:

> The Eastern Orthodox Church insists on reading human nature in dual rather than singular terms, taking seriously the Hebrew doublet which declares that we are made in "God's image and likeness." For the Orthodox, the image of God remains in us virtually indestructible. (Wood 2014)

> [B]ut after the fall they [Adam and Eve] were estranged from their creator and subject to pain, sorrow, and death. Deification, then, is the restoration of the divine likeness that humanity lost along with its beauty, purity, and incorruption. (Jensen 2007)

Francis J. Caponi, O.S.A. and Ralph Wood compare Lewis's distinction between "nearness by likeness" and "nearness by approach" (Lewis 1960b: 15) with the Orthodox distinction between "image" and "likeness" (Caponi 2010: 69; Wood 2014). In *The Four Loves*, Lewis's nearness by likeness corresponds to the Orthodox understanding of image, and nearness by approach to the Orthodox view of likeness:

> We must distinguish two things which might both possibly be called "nearness to God." One is likeness to God. God has impressed some sort of likeness to Himself, I suppose, in all that He has made. . . . Man has a more important likeness . . . by being rational. Angels, we believe, have likenesses which Man lacks: immortality and intuitive knowledge. In that way all men, whether good or bad, all angels including those that fell, are more like God than the animals are. Their natures are in this sense "nearer" to the Divine Nature. But, secondly, there is what we may call nearness of approach. If this is what we mean, the states in which man is "nearest" to God are those in which he is most surely and swiftly approaching his final union with God, vision of God and enjoyment of God. (Lewis 1960b: 15)

All who approach God, do so only because God has first approached them. "When you come to knowing God, the initiative lies on His side. If He does not show Himself, nothing you can do will enable you to find Him" (2001b: 164).

While God takes the initiative, He awaits the creature's permission:

> He [Christ] warned people to "count the cost" before becoming Christians. "Make no mistake," He says, "if you let me, I will make you perfect. The

moment you put yourself in My hands, that is what you are in for.... You have free will, and if you choose, you can push Me away. But if you do not push Me away, understand that I am going to see this job through.... I will never rest, nor let you rest, until you are literally perfect – until My Father can say without reservation that He is well pleased with you, as He said He was well pleased with Me. (2001b: 202)

We see a picture of this kind of permission in *The Great Divorce*. There a ghost, on a day trip from Hell to Heaven, bothered and beleaguered by a reptile representing lust, is approached by an angel who offers to kill the creature. The angel knows that the ghost will have no peace while the reptile lives. The angel also knows that deliverance depends upon the ghost's free choice: "I cannot kill it against your will. It is impossible. Have I your permission?" (1946: 100). In response to the ghost's trepidation, "How can I tell you to kill it? You'd kill *me* if you did," the angel answers, "It is not so," and then adds, "I never said it wouldn't hurt you. I said it wouldn't kill you" (100).

When a creature freely gives up its natural life, its self-centeredness (2001b: 178), and draws near to Christ, it begins to receive "the good infection" or "*Zoe*" (176, 177, 181, 221). "He [Christ] came into the created universe, of His own will, bringing with him the Zoe, the new life.... Everyone who gets it gets it by personal contact with Him" (221). Contact comes through baptism, belief, and Holy Communion (61), prayer (161–62, 176, 187–8), other Christians (165, 190); "dressing up as Christ" or "good pretending" (187–8). The transformation from a mere creature to a son of God (220), which Lewis compared to "turning a tin soldier into a real little man" (179) and "turning a horse into a winged creature" (116), is not accomplished in this lifetime (204, 207). It cannot be, for physical death is required for the transformation (207). Beyond that, in his last work *Letters to Malcolm*, a fictional correspondence, the Lewis character wrote "I believe in Purgatory.... Our souls *demand* Purgatory, don't they?" (1964: 108).

The transformed creature will be "a little Christ" (2001b: 177, 192, 199, 225), a *son* of God (181), but never a *Son* of God: "All Christians are agreed that there is, in the full and original sense, only one 'Son of God'" (183). "What God begets is God; just as what man begets is man. What God creates is not God; just as what man makes is not man. That is why men are not Sons of God in the sense that Christ is" (157–58). Becoming a son of God is not the end of individuality but its true beginning, "It is when I turn to Christ, when I give myself up to His Personality, that I first begin to have a real personality of my own" (226). Each son of God, each little Christ, "shall forever know and praise some one aspect of the Divine beauty better than any other creature can" (2001d: 154). Even so, there could never be enough "little Christs" to adequately express the grandeur of God:

"There is so much of Him that millions and millions of 'little Christs,' all different, will still be too few to express Him fully" (2001b: 225).

For Further Reading: David Merconi argues that "the unifying lens through which every page of *Mere Christianity* is best read, is the divination of the human person in Christ" (Merconi 2017: 3). Myk Habets applies "the concept of 'Transposition' to Lewis's doctrine of *theosis*" to allow "an investigation into possible ways in which the discussion of *theosis* may be extended" (2010). On the place of theosis in the Anglican tradition, see Allchin (1988). Humphrey (2017) provides an Orthodox perspective on Lewis's theology. Wayne Martindale (2005) finds in Lewis's fiction corrections of caricatures of heaven and hell. Jerry L. Walls (2012: 153–176) discusses Lewis's view of purgatory. In his work, *The Lion's Country*, Charlie W. Starr includes in chapter 10, "Lewis's Vision of Heaven," a hitherto unpublished excerpt from "Lewis's Prayer Manuscript" (Starr 2022: 113–160).

References

Aldwinkle, Stella (2015). Memories of the Socratic Club. In Roger White, Judith Wolfe, and Brendan N. Wolfe, eds., *C.S. Lewis and His Circle: Essays and Memoirs from the Oxford C.S. Lewis Society*, Oxford: Oxford University Press, 192–194.

Alexander, Samuel (2020). *Space, Time and Deity: The Gifford Lectures at Glasgow 1916–1918*, London: Macmillan.

Allchin, A. M. (1988). *Participation in God: A Forgotten Strand in Anglican Tradition*, Wilton, CT: Morehouse.

Anderson, Trevor (2016/2017). C.S. Lewis and Penal Substitution: A Problem Case for New Calvinist Theology. *The Evangelical Quarterly*, 88 (4), 285–304.

Anscombe, G. E. M. (1981). *The Collected Philosophical Papers of G.E.M. Anscombe: II Metaphysics and Philosophy of Mind*, Minneapolis, MN: University of Minnesota Press.

Anscombe, G. E. M. (2015). C.S. Lewis's Rewrite of Chapter III of *Miracles*. In Roger White, Judith Wolfe, and Brendan N. Wolfe, eds., *C.S. Lewis and His Circle: Essays and Memoirs from the Oxford C.S. Lewis Society*, Oxford: Oxford University Press, 15–23.

Anscombe, G. E. M. (2019). Some Remarks on C.S. Lewis's *Reflections on the Psalms* (1959). *Journal of Inklings Studies*, 9 (2), 176–177.

Anselm, Saint (1998). *Proslogion*. In Brian Davies and G. R. Evans, eds., M. J. Charlesworth, trans., *Anselm of Canterbury: The Major Works*, Oxford: Oxford University Press. 82–104

Armstrong, Christopher (2016). *Medieval Wisdom for Modern Christians: Finding Authentic Faith in a Forgotten Age with C.S. Lewis*, Grand Rapids, MI: Brazos Press.

Athanasius, Saint (1946). *On the Incarnation*, Sister Penelope Lawson, ed. and trans., New York: Macmillan.

Augustine, Saint (1961). *Confessions*, R. S. Pine, trans., Middlesex: Penguin Books.

Babbage, Stuart Barton (1980). To the Royal Air Force. In Carolyn Keefe, ed., *C.S. Lewis Speaker & Teacher*, Grand Rapids, MI: Zondervan, 65–76.

Baggett, David (2015a). Pro: The Moral Argument is Convincing. In Gregory Bassham, ed., *C.S. Lewis's Christian Apologetics: Pro and Con*, Leiden, NL: Brill Rodopi, 121–140.

Baggett, David (2015b). Reply to Erik Wielenberg. In Gregory Bassham, ed., *C.S. Lewis's Christian Apologetics: Pro and Con*, Leiden, NL: Brill Rodopi, 153–162.

Baggett, David and Jerry Walls (2019). *The Moral Argument: A History*, Oxford: Oxford University Press.

Balfour, Arthur J. (2000). *Theism and Humanism: The Book that Influenced C.S. Lewis*, Michael W. Perry, ed., Seattle, WA: Inklings Books.

Barkman, Adam (2009). *C.S. Lewis & Philosophy as a Way of Life: A Comprehensive Historical Examination of His Philosophical Thoughts*, Allentown, PA: Zossima Press.

Barkman, Adam (2011). "No Doubt They are Substantially Right": C.S. Lewis and the Calvinists. *Inklings–Jarbuch*, 29, 8–28.

Barkman, Adam (2015a). Con: C.S. Lewis's Trilemma: Case Not Proven. In Gregory Bassham, ed., *C.S. Lewis's Christian Apologetics: Pro and Con*, Leiden, NL: Brill Rodopi, 191–199.

Barkman, Adam (2015b). Reply to Donald Williams. In Gregory Bassham, ed., *C.S. Lewis's Christian Apologetics: Pro and Con*, Leiden, NL: Brill Rodopi, 205–210.

Bassham, Gregory (2015a). Con: Quenching the Argument from Desire. In Gregory Bassham, ed., *C.S. Lewis's Christian Apologetics: Pro and Con*, Leiden, NL: Brill Rodopi, 454–455.

Bassham, Gregory (2015b). Reply to Peter S. Williams. In Gregory Bassham, ed., *C.S. Lewis's Christian Apologetics: Pro and Con*, Leiden, NL: Brill Rodopi, 69–74.

Bauckham, Richard (2013). Are We Still Missing the Elephant? C.S. Lewis's "Fernseed and Elephants" a Half Century on. *Theology*, 116 (6), 427–434.

Bauckham, Richard (2017). *Jesus and the Eyewitnesses: The Gospels as Eyewitness Testimony*, 2nd ed, Grand Rapids, MI: William B. Eerdmans.

Baynes, Leslie (2017). C.S. Lewis's Use of Scripture in the "Liar, Lunatic, Lord" Argument. *Journal of Inklings Studies*, 4 (2), 27–66.

Beversluis, John (2007). *C.S. Lewis and the Search for Rational Religion*, rev., updated, Amherst, NY:Prometheus Books.

Beyer, Douglas (2006). From Kenosis to Theosis: Reflections on the Views of C.S. Lewis. *Inklings Forever: Published Colloquium Proceedings 1997–2016*, 5 (18), 90–95.

Blomberg, Craig L. (1987). *The Historical Reliability of the Gospels*, Downers Grove, IL: InterVarsity Press.

Blomberg, Craig L. (2001). *The Historical Reliability of John's Gospel*, Downers Grove, IL: InterVarsity Press.

Bowman Jr. , Robert M. and J. Edward Komoszewski (2007). *Putting Jesus in His Place: The Case for the Deity of Christ*, Grand Rapids, MI: Kregel.

Brazier, Paul H. (2012). *C. S. Lewis–The Work of Christ Revealed*. Eugene, OR: Pickwick.

Brown, Devin (2013). *A Life Observed: A Spiritual Biography of C.S. Lewis*, Grand Rapids, MI: Brazos Press.

Brown, Devin (2015). Are the Chronicles of Narnia Sexist? In Carolyn Curtis and Mary Pomroy Key, eds., *Women and C.S. Lewis: What His Life and Literature Reveal for Today's Culture*, Oxford: Lion Books, 93–108.

Burson, Scott R. and Jerry L. Walls (1998). *C.S. Lewis & Francis Schaeffer: Lessons for a New Century from the Most Influential Apologists of Our Time*, Downers Grove, IL: InterVarsity Press.

Caponi, Francis J. (2010). Gods and Friends: C.S. Lewis on Divinization. *Expositions*, 4 (1&2), 63–79.

Coghill, Neville (1965). The Approach to English. In Jocelyn Gibb, ed., *Light on C.S. Lewis*, New York: Harcourt Brace Jovanovich, 51–66.

Davis, Stephen T. (2004). The Mad/Bad/God Trilemma: A Reply to Daniel Howard-Snyder. *Faith and Philosophy: Journal of the Society of Christian Philosophers*, 21 (4), 480–492.

Davis, Stephen T. (2009). *Disputed Issues: Contending for Christian Faith in Today's Academic Setting*, Waco, TX: Baylor University Press.

Depoe, John M. (2014). The Self-Defeat of Naturalism: A Critical Comparison of Alvin Plantinga and C.S. Lewis. *Christian Scholar's Review*, 64 (1), https://christianscholars.com/the-self-defeat-of-naturalism-a-critical-com parison-of-alvin-plantinga-and-c-s-lewis/.

Derrick, Stephanie L. (2018). *The Fame of C.S. Lewis: A Controversialist's Reception in Britain and America*, Oxford: Oxford University Press.

Descartes, René (1984). Meditations on First Philosophy, John Cottingham, trans. In John Cottingham, Robert Stoothoff, and Dugald Murdoch (eds. and trans.) *The Philosophical Writings of Descartes, Vol. II*, Cambridge: Cambridge University Press.

Dorsett, Lyle W. (2004). *Seeking the Secret Place: The Spiritual Formation of C.S. Lewis*, Grand Rapids, MI: Brazos Press.

Downing, David C. (2002). *The Most Reluctant Convert: C.S. Lewis's Journey to Faith*, Downers Grove, IL: InterVarsity Press.

Duriez, Colin (2005). *The C.S. Lewis Chronicles: The Indispensable Biography of the Creator of Narnia Full of Little-Known Facts, Events and Miscellany*, London: Darton, Longman and Todd.

Duriez, Colin (2015a). *Bedeviled: Lewis, Tolkien and the Shadow of Evil*, Downers Grove, IL: InterVarsity Press.

Duriez, Colin (2015b). *The Oxford Inklings: Lewis, Tolkien and Their Circle*, Oxford: Lion Books.

Euripides (2001). *Hippolytus*, Michael R. Halleran, ed. and trans., Newbury MA: Focus Classical Library.

Gilmore, Charles (2005). To the RAF. In James T. Como, ed., *Remembering C. S. Lewis: Recollections of Those Who Knew Him*, San Francisco, CA: Ignatius Press, 309–316.

Goetz, Stewart (2013). The Argument from Reason. *Philosophia Christi*, 15 (1), 47–62.

Goetz, Stewart (2018). *C.S. Lewis*, Oxford: Wiley-Blackwell.

Griffiths, Alan Bede (2005). The Adventure of Faith. In James T. Como, ed., *Remembering C. S. Lewis: Recollections of Those Who Knew Him*, San Francisco, CA: Ignatious Press, 76–95.

Gyler, Diana Pavlac (2007). *The Company They Keep: C.S. Lewis and J.R.R. Tolkien as Writers in Community*, Kent, OH: The Kent State University Press.

Habets, Myk (2010). Walking in *mirabilibus supra me*: How C.S. Lewis transposes *theosis*. *Evangelical Quarterly*, 82 (1), 15–27.

Hebblethwaite, Brian (1987). *The Incarnation: Collected Essays in Christology*, Cambridge: Cambridge University Press.

Heck, Joel D. (2005). *Irrigating Deserts: C.S. Lewis on Education*, St. Louis, MO: Concordia Publishing House.

Heck, Joel D. (2017). *From Atheism to Christianity: The Story of C.S. Lewis*, St. Lewis, MO: Concordia Publishing House.

Heck, Joel D. (2021). *No Ordinary People: 21 Friendships of C.S. Lewis*, Hamden, CT: Winged Lion Press.

Heck, Joel D. (2022a). The Complete Works of C.S. Lewis. *Joel Heck's Website*, May 13. www.joelheck.com/resorces/TheCompleteWorksofCSLewis.pdf (Accessed November 18, 2022).

Heck, Joel D. (2022b). Chronologically Lewis, *Joel Heck's Website*, October 18. www.joelheck.com/chronologically-lewis.php (Accessed November 18, 2022).

Hinton, Marvin D. (1998). The Weight of Glory. In Jeffrey D. Schultz and John G. West Jr., eds., *The C.S. Lewis Reader's Encyclopedia*, Grand Rapids, MI: Zondervan, 423.

Holyer, Robert (1988). The Argument from Desire. *Faith and Philosophy*, 5 (1), 61–71.

Hooper, W. (1996). *C.S. Lewis Companion & Guide*, New York, NY: HarperCollins.

Honeycutt, Willie (2017). True Myth in the Apologetics of C.S. Lewis. In David Baggett, Gary R. Habermas, and Jerry L. Walls, eds., *C. S. Lewis as Philosopher: Truth, Goodness, and Beauty*, Lynchburg, VA: Liberty University Press, 105–127.

Hooper, Walter (1996). *C.S. Lewis Companion & Guide*, New York, NY: HarperCollins.

Hooper, Walter (2005a). A Bibliography of the Writings of C.S. Lewis: Revised and Enlarged. In James T. Como, ed., *Remembering C.S. Lewis: Recollections of Those Who Knew Him*, San Francisco, CA: Ignatius Press, 387–473.

Hooper, Walter (2005b). Oxford's Bonny Fighter. In James T. Como, ed., *Remembering C.S. Lewis: Recollections of Those Who Knew Him*, San Francisco, CA: Ignatius Press, 241–308.

Hooper, Walter (2015). It All Began with a Picture: The Making of C.S. Lewis's Chronicles of Narnia. In Roger White, Judith Wolfe, Brendan Wolff, eds., *C. S. Lewis & His Circle: Essays and Memoirs from the Oxford C.S. Lewis Society*, Oxford: Oxford University Press, 150–163.

Houston, James M. (1989). The Prayer Life of C.S. Lewis. In Michael H. Macdonald and Andrew A. Tadie, eds., *The Riddle of Joy: G. K. Chesterton and C.S. Lewis*, Grand Rapids, MI: William B. Eerdmans, 69–86.

Howard-Snyder, Daniel (2004). Was Jesus Mad, Bad, or God? . . . or Merely Mistaken? *Faith and Philosophy, Journal of the Society of Christian Philosophers*, 21 (4), 456–479.

Humphrey, Edith M. (2017). *Further up and Further in: Orthodox Conversations with C.S. Lewis on Scripture & Theology*, Yonkers, NY: St. Vladimir's Seminary Press.

Hyles, Vernon R. (1992). Campbell and the Inklings – Tolkien, Lewis, and Williams. In Kenneth L. Golden, ed., *Uses of Comparative Mythology: Essays on the Work of Joseph Campbell*, New York: Garland.

Jensen, Chris (2007). Shine as the Sun: C.S. Lewis and the Doctrine of Deification. In *Pursuit of Truth: A Journal of Christian Scholarship*, October 31. www.cslewis.org/journal/shine-as-the-sun-cs-lewis-and-the-doctrine-of-deification/ (Accessed November 18, 2022).

Johnson, Adam J. (2022). Silent No More: Lewis's Cosmological View of Christ's Atoning Work. In Bruce R. Johnson, ed., *The Undiscovered C.S. Lewis: Essays in Memory of Christopher W. Mitchell*, Hamden, CT: Winged Lion Press, 215–238.

Johnson, David Kyle (2015a). Con: Naturalism Undefeated. In Gregory Bassham, ed., *C.S. Lewis's Christian Apologetics: Pro and Con*, Leiden, NL: Brill Rodopi, 91–103.

Johnson, David Kyle (2015b). Reply to Victor Reppert. In Gregory Bassham, ed., *C.S. Lewis's Christian Apologetics: Pro and Con*, Leiden, NL: Brill Rodopi, 113–119.

Johnson, David Kyle (2018). Retiring the Argument from Reason: Another Response to Victor Reppert. *Philosophia Christi*, 20 (2), 541–563.

Just, Felix (2018). "I Am" Sayings in the Fourth Gospel, *Introductory Materials for the Fourth Gospel*, April 11. www.catholic-resources.org/John/Themes-IAM.htm (Accessed November 18, 2022).

Kreeft, Peter J. (1989). Lewis's Argument from Desire. In Michael H. Macdonald and Andrew A. Tadie, eds., *G.K. Chesterton and C.S. Lewis: The Riddle of Joy*, Grand Rapids, MI: William B. Eerdmans, 249–272.

Lee, Robert Sloan (2017). As If Swallowing Light Itself: C.S. Lewis's Argument from Desire, Part I. In David Baggett, Gary R. Habermas, and Jerry L. Walls, eds., *C. S. Lewis as Philosopher: Truth, Goodness, and Beauty*, Lynchburg, VA: Liberty University Press, 315–326.

Lewis, C.S. (1942). *Broadcast Talks*, London: Geoffrey Bles.

Lewis, C. S. (1944). *Beyond Personality: The Christian Idea of God*, London: Geoffrey Bles.

Lewis, C. S. (1946). *The Great Divorce*, New York: Macmillan.

Lewis, C. S. (1947). *Miracles: A Preliminary Study*, 1st ed., New York: Macmillan.

Lewis, C. S. (1955a). *The Abolition of Man*, New York: MacMillan.

Lewis, C. S. (1955b). *Surprised by Joy: The Shape of My Early Life*, New York: Harcourt Brace & World.

Lewis, C. S. (1958a). *The Allegory of Love*, London: Oxford University Press.

Lewis, C. S. (1958b). *The Pilgrim's Regress: An Allegorical Apology for Christianity Reason and Romanticism*, Grand Rapids, MI: William B. Eerdmans.

Lewis, C. S. (1960a). *An Experiment in Criticism*, Cambridge: Cambridge University Press.

Lewis, C. S. (1960b). *The Four Loves*, New York: Harcourt, Brace, Jovanovich.

Lewis, C. S. (1961). *A Preface to Paradise Lost*, London: Oxford University Press.

Lewis, C. S. (1964). *Letters to Malcolm: Chiefly on Prayer*, New York: Harcourt Brace Jovanovich.

Lewis, C. S. (1965a). *Out of the Silent Planet*, New York: MacMillan.

Lewis, C. S. (1965b). *Perelandra*, New York: Macmillan.

Lewis, C. S. (1965c). *That Hideous Strength: A Modern Fairy-Tale for Grown-ups*, New York: Macmillan.

Lewis, C. S. (1966). *Til We Have Faces*, Grand Rapids, MI: William B. Eerdmans.

Lewis, C. S. (1967a). *Christian Reflections* Walter Hooper, ed., Grand Rapids, MI: William B. Eerdmans.

Lewis, C. S. (1967b). *The Discarded Image*, Cambridge: Cambridge University Press.

Lewis, C. S. (1970). *God in the Dock*, Grand Rapids, MI: William B. Eerdmans.

Lewis, C. S. (1974). *Studies in Words*, London: Cambridge University Press.

Lewis, C. S. (1979). *Selected Literary Essays*, New York: Cambridge University Press.

Lewis, C. S. (1980). *The Weight of Glory and Other Addresses*, New York: Macmillan.

Lewis, C. S. (1982). *On Stories and Other Essays on Literature*, Walter Hooper ed., New York: Harcourt Brace Jovanovich.

Lewis, C. S. (1986a). *Present Concerns: Essays by C.S. Lewis*, Walter Hooper, ed., San Diego, CA: Harcourt Brace Jovanovich.

Lewis, C. S. (1986b). *Reflections on the Psalms*, San Diego, CA: Harcourt.

Lewis, C. S. (1992). *All My Road before Me: The Diary of C.S. Lewis, (1922–1927)*, San Diego, CA: Harcourt Brace Janovich.

Lewis, C. S. (2000a). *The Lion, the Witch, and the Wardrobe*, New York: HarperCollins.

Lewis, C. S. (2000b). *The Silver Chair*, New York: HarperCollins.

Lewis, C. S. (2001a). *A Grief Observed*, New York: HarperCollins.

Lewis, C. S. (2001b). *Mere Christianity*, New York: HarperCollins.

Lewis, C. S. (2001c). *Miracles: A Preliminary Study*, New York: HarperCollins.

Lewis, C. S. (2001d). *The Problem of Pain*, New York: HarperCollins

Lewis, C. S. (2001e). *The Screwtape Letters*, New York: HarperCollins

Lewis, C. S. (2004a). *The Collected Letters of C.S. Lewis*, HarperCollins New York, NY. *Volume I: Family Letters 1905–1931*, Walter Hooper, ed., HarperSanFrancisco.

Lewis, C. S. (2004b). *The Collected Letters of C.S. Lewis*, HarperCollins New York, NY. *Volume II: Books, Broadcasts, and the War 1931–1949*, Walter Hooper, ed., HarperSanFrancisco.

Lewis, C. S. (2007). *The Collected Letters of C.S. Lewis*, HarperCollins New York, NY. *Volume III: Narnia, Cambridge, and Joy 1950–1963*, Walter Hooper, ed., HarperSanFrancisco.

Lewis, C. S. (2008). *Yours, Jack: Spiritual Direction from C.S. Lewis*, HarperCollins New York, NY. Paul F. Ford, ed., HarperOne.

Lewis C. S. (2013). "Early Prose Joy": C.S. Lewis's Early Draft of an Autobiographical Manuscript. *VII An Anglo-American Literary Review*, 30 (2), 13–49.

Lewis, C. S. (2014). *The Pilgrim's Regress: Wade Annotated Edition*, David C. Downing, ed., intro, Grand Rapids, MI: William B. Eerdmans.

Lewis, C. S. (2015). *The Collected Poems of C.S. Lewis: A Critical Edition*, Don King, ed., Kent, OH: Kent State University Press.

Lewis, C. S. (2017). *The World's Last Night and Other Essays*, New York: HarperOne.

Lewis, C. S. (2022). *English Literature in the Sixteenth Century: Excluding Drama*, New York: HarperOne.

Lovell, Steven Jon James (2003). Philosophical Themes From C.S. Lewis, Unpublished Ph.D. Thesis, University of Sheffield. https://etheses.white rose.ac.uk/6054/1/398641.pdf.

MacDonald, George (1964). Phantastes: A Faerie Romance. In *Phantastes and Lilith*, Grand Rapids, MI: William B. Eerdmans, 13–182.

MacDonald, George (1970). *George MacDonald: An Anthology*, C.S. Lewis, ed., London: Geoffrey Bles.

Manning, Jr. Gary (2015). Does "I Am" Always Refer to God in the Gospel of John? The Good Book Blog: Talbot School of Theology Faculty Blog, September 21.www.biola.edu/blogs/good-book-blog/2015/does-i-am-always-refer-to-god-in-the-gospel-of-john (Accessed November 18, 2022).

Marsden, George M. (2016). *C.S. Lewis's Mere Christianity: A Biography*, Princeton, NJ: Princeton University Press.

Martindale, Wayne (2005). *Beyond the Shadowlands: C.S. Lewis on Heaven and Hell*, Wheaton, IL: Crossway.

McGrath, Alister (2002). *In the Beginning: The Story of the King James Bible and How it Changed a Nation, a Language, and a Culture*. New York, NY: Anchor.

McGrath, Alister (2013). *C.S. Lewis – A Life: Eccentric Genius, Reluctant Prophet*, Carol Stream, IL: Tyndale House.

McGrath, Alister E. (2014). *The Intellectual World of C.S. Lewis*, Oxford: Wiley–Blackwell.

McGrath, Alister (2019). *Richard Dawkins, C.S. Lewis and the Meaning of Life*, London: Society for Promoting Christian Knowledge.

Menzies, James (2014). *True Myth: C. S. Lewis and Joseph Campbell on the Veracity of Christianity*, Eugene OR: Pickwick.

Merconi, David (2017). Mere Christianity: Theosis the British Way. *Journal of Inklings Study*, 4 (1), 3–18.

Mitchell, Christopher W. (1997). University Battles: C.S. Lewis and the Oxford University Socratic Club. In Angus J. L. Menuge, ed., *C.S. Lewis Lightbearer in the Shadowlands: The Evangelistic Vision of C.S. Lewis*, Wheaton, IL: Crossway Books, 329–351.

Morris, Thomas V. (1986). *The Logic of God Incarnate*, Ithaca, NY: Cornell University Press.

Neal, Mark and Jerry Root (2020). *The Neglected Lewis: Exploring the Riches of His Most Overlooked Books*, Brewster, MA: Mount Tabor Books.

Oden, Thomas C. (2001a). *The Living God: Systematic Theology: Volume One*, Peabody, MA: Prince Press.

Oden, Thomas C. (2001b). *The Word of Life: Systematic Theology: Volume Two*, Peabody, MA: Prince Press.

Oden, Thomas C. (2001c). *Life in the Spirit: Systematic Theology: Volume Three*, Peabody, MA: Prince Press.

Pascal, Blaise (1966). *Pensées*, A. J. Krailsheimer, trans., Harmondsworth, New York, NY, Middlesex: Penguin Books.

Peterson, Michael (2017). C.S. Lewis on the Necessity of Gratuitous Evil. In David Baggett, Gary R. Habermas, and Jerry L. Walls, eds., *C. S. Lewis as Philosopher: Truth, Goodness, and Beauty*, Lynchburg, VA: Liberty University Press, 211–228.

Peterson, Michael L. (2020). *C.S. Lewis and the Christian Worldview*, Oxford: Oxford University Press.

Phillips, Justin (2002). *C.S. Lewis in a Time of War: The World War II Broadcasts That Riveted a Nation and Became the Classic Mere Christianity*, New York: Harper Collins.

Plantinga, Alvin (1977). *God, Freedom, and Evil*, Grand Rapids, MI: William B. Eerdmans.

Plantinga, Alvin (2011). *Where the Conflict Really Lies*, Oxford: Oxford University Press.

Plato (1961). *Euthyphro*. In Edith Hamilton and Huntington Cairns (eds.), Lane Cooper, (tans.), *Plato: The Collected Dialogues Including the Letters*, Bollingen Series LXXI, Princeton NJ: Princeton University Press, 169–185.

Poe, Harry Lee (2019). *Becoming C.S. Lewis: A Biography of Young Jack Lewis (1898–1918)*, Wheaton, IL: Crossway.

Poe, Harry Lee (2021). *The Making of C.S. Lewis: From Atheist to Apologist (1918–1945)*, Wheaton, IL: Crossway.

Poe, Harry Lee (2022). *The Completion of C.S. Lewis: From War to Joy (1945–1963)*, Wheaton, IL: Crossway.

Purtill, Richard L. (2006). *Lord of the Elves and Eldils: Fantasy and Philosophy in C.S. Lewis and J.R.R. Tolkien*, 2nd ed., San Francisco, CA: Ignatius Press.

Rainbow, Paul A. (2014). *Johannine Theology: The Gospel, the Epistles and the Apocalypse*, Downers Grove, IL: InterVarsity Press.

Reppert, Victor (2003). *C.S. Lewis's Dangerous Idea: In Defense of the Argument from Reason*, Downers Grove: IL: InterVarsity Press.

Reppert, Victor (2015a). Pro: The Argument from Reason Defended. In Gregory Bassham, ed., *C.S. Lewis's Christian Apologetics: Pro and Con*, Leiden, NL: Brill Rodopi, 75–89.

Reppert, Victor (2015b). Reply to David Kyle Johnson. In Gregory Bassham, ed., *C.S. Lewis's Christian Apologetics: Pro and Con*, Leiden, NL: Brill Rodopi, 105–111.

Reppert, Victor (2018). Extending the Debate on the Argument from Reason a Further Response to David K. Johnson. *Philosophia Christi*, 20 (2) 517–539.

Rigney, Joe (2018). *Lewis on the Christian Life: Becoming Truly Human in the Presence of God*, Wheaton, IL: Crossway Press.

Root, Jerry (2009). *C. S. Lewis and a Problem of Evil: An Investigation of a Pervasive Theme*, Eugene, OR: Pickwick.

Ross, Charles Stanley (2012). C.S. Lewis, Augustine, and the Rhythm of the Trinity. *Journal of Inklings Studies*, 2 (1), 3–22.

Ryken, Leland and Marjorie Lamp Mead (2005). *A Reader's Guide Through the Wardrobe: Exploring C.S. Lewis's Classic Story*, Downers Grove, IL: InterVarsity Press.

Sayers, Dorothy L. (1943). *The Man Born to be King: A Play-Cycle on the Life of Our Lord and Savior Jesus Christ*, San Francisco, CA: Ignatius Press.

Schakel, Peter J. (1980). *Reading with the Heart: The Way into Narnia*, Grand Rapids, MI: William B. Eerdmans.

Simek, Slater (2022). A Bayesian Exploration of C.S. Lewis's Argument from Desire. *Sophia*, https://doi.org/10.1007/s11841-021-00887-9.

Starr, Charlie W. (2022). *The Lion's Country: C.S. Lewis's Theory of the Real*, Kent, OH: Kent State University Press.

Swinburne, Richard (1994). *The Christian God*, Oxford: Oxford University Press.

Taliaferro, Charles (1998). *Praying with C.S. Lewis*, Winona, MN: Saint Mary's Press Christian Brothers.

Taliaferro, Charles (2010). On Naturalism. In Robert MacSwain and Michael Ward, eds., *The Cambridge Companion to C.S. Lewis*, Cambridge: Cambridge University Press, 105–118.

Taliaferro, Charles (2015). Arthur James Balfour, Theism and Humanism. In David Werther and Susan Werther, eds., *C.S. Lewis's List: The Ten Books That Influenced Him Most*, New York: Bloomsbury Academic, 201–217.

Taliaferro, Charles (2022). *A Narnian Vision of the Atonement: A Defense of the Ransom Theory*, Eugene, OR: Cascade Books.

Tallon, Philip (2015). Pro: The Problem of Pain Defended. In Gregory Bassham, ed., *C.S. Lewis's Christian Apologetics: Pro and Con*, Leiden, NL: Brill Rodopi, 211–225.

Tolkien, Christopher (1988). Preface. In J. R. R. Tolkien, ed., *Tree and Leaf*, London: HarperCollins, v–ix.

Tolkien, J. R. R. (1988). *Tree and Leaf*, London: HarperCollins.

Trudeau, George Harold (2021). Synthesizing True Myth and Jungian Criticism: Jordan Peterson, Carl Jung, and C.S. Lewis in Conversation. *Heythrop Journal,* LXII, 863–875.

Vanderhorst, Ariel James (2009). Mere Atonement: C.S. Lewis & the Multiple Angles of Redemption. *Touchstone: A Journal of Mere Christianity*, 22 (3). www.touchstonemag.com/archives/article.php?id=22-03-027-f.

Vaus, Will (2004). *Mere Theology*, Downers Grove, IL: InterVarsity Press.

Vaus, Will (2014). *C.S. Lewis's Top Ten: Influential Books and Authors, Volume One*, Hamden, CT: Winged Lion Press.

Vaus, Will (2015). *C.S. Lewis's Top Ten: Influential Books and Authors, Volume Two*, Hamden, CT: Winged Lion Press.

Vaus, Will (2018). *C.S. Lewis's Top Ten: Influential Books and Authors, Volume Three*, Hamden, CT: Winged Lion Press.

Walls, Jerry L. (2012). *Purgatory: The Logic of Total Transformation*, Oxford: Oxford University Press.

Ward, Michael (2021). *After Humanity: A Guide to C.S. Lewis's The Abolition of Man*, Park Ridge, IL: Word on Fire Academic.

Ware, Kallistos (1998). God of the Fathers: C.S. Lewis and Eastern Christianity. In David Mills, ed., *The Pilgrim's Guide: C.S. Lewis and the Art of Witness*, Grand Rapids, MI: William B. Eerdmans, 53–69.

Werther, David and Susan Werther, eds. (2015). *C.S. Lewis's List: The Ten Books that Influenced Him Most*, New York: Bloomsbury Academic.

Wielenberg, Erik J. (2008). *God and the Reach of Reason*: C.S. Lewis, David Hume, and Bertrand Russell, Cambridge: Cambridge University Press.

Wielenberg, Erik J. (2015a). Con: A Critique of the Moral Argument. In Gregory Bassham, ed., *C.S. Lewis's Christian Apologetics: Pro and Con*, Leiden, NL: Brill Rodopi, 141–151.

Wielenberg, Erik J. (2015b). Reply to David Baggett. In Gregory Bassham, ed., *C.S. Lewis's Christian Apologetics: Pro and Con*, Leiden, NL: Brill Rodopi, 163–169.

Williams, Charles (1950). *The Place of the Lion*, Grand Rapids, MI: William B. Eerdmans.

Williams, Donald (2017). Made for Another World. *Philosophia Christi*, 19 (21), 449–454.

Williams, Donald S. (2015a). Pro: A Defense of Lewis's "Trilemma." In Gregory Bassham, ed., *C.S. Lewis's Christian Apologetics: Pro and Con*, Leiden, NL: Brill Rodopi, 171–189.

Williams, Donald S. (2015b). Reply to Adam Barkman. In Gregory Bassham, ed., *C.S. Lewis's Christian Apologetics: Pro and Con*, Leiden, NL: Brill Rodopi, 2001–2004.

Williams, Donald T. (2007). An Apologist's Evening Prayer: Reflecting on C.S. Lewis's *Reflections on the Psalms*. In Bruce L. Edwards, ed., *C.S. Lewis Life, Works, Legacy, Vol. 3, Apologist, Philosopher & Theologian*, Westport, CT: Praeger Press, 237–256.

Williams, Donald T. (2016). *Deeper Magic: The Theology behind the Writings of C.S. Lewis*, Baltimore, MD: Square Halo Press.

Williams, Peter S. (2015a). Pro: A Defense of C.S. Lewis's Argument from Desire. In Gregory Bassham, ed., *C.S. Lewis's Christian Apologetics: Pro and Con*, Leiden, NL: Brill Rodopi, 27–44.

Williams, Peter S. (2015b). Reply to Gregory Bassham. In Gregory Bassham, ed., *C.S. Lewis's Christian Apologetics: Pro and Con*, Leiden, NL: Brill Rodopi, 57–68.

Williams, Peter S. (2016). Defending Arguments from Desire: A Second Response to Gregory Bassham. www.peterswilliams.com/wp-content/uploads/2016/11/In-Defence-of-Arguments-from-Desire_v4.pdf.

Wilson, Douglas (2014). Undragoned. In John Piper and David Mathis, eds., *The Romantic Rationalist*, Wheaton, IL: Crossway, 65–80.

Wood, Ralph C. (2014). Becoming Icons of God: Divinization in the Writings of C.S. Lewis. *ABC: Religion and Ethics*, 18. www.abc.net.au/religion/becoming-icons-of-god-divinization-in-the-writings-of-cs-lewis/10099390 (Accessed: November 18, 2022).

Wright, N. T. (1996). *Jesus and the Victory of God: Christian Origins and the Question of God, Vol. 2*, Minneapolis, MN: Fortress Press.

Wright, N. T. (1998). Jesus and the Identity of God. *N.T. Wright Page*. https://ntwrightpage.com/2016/07/12/jesus-and-the-identity-of-god/ (Accessed November 21, 2022).

Wright, N. T. (2001). *Mark for Everyone*, Louisville, KY: Westminster John Knox Press.

Zaleski, Philip and Carol Zaleski (2015). *The Fellowship: The Literary Lives of the Inklings: J.R.R. Tolkien, C.S. Lewis, Owen Barfield, Charles Williams*, New York: Farrar, Straus and Giroux.

Acknowledgments

I wish to express my thanks to Michael L. Peterson for the invitation to write this volume; my wife Susan for her supererogatory support and editorial excellence; my mother Betty for her encouragement; Mark Linville (Uncle W) for his many helpful comments and questions; Paul Rainbow for his wise counsel and careful reading, as well as to the two anonymous reviewers. Special thanks go to Laura Schmidt of the Wade Center at Wheaton College for her assistance with documentation, and to the C.S. Lewis Society of Madison for stimulating discussions.

Cambridge Elements ☰

The Problems of God

Series Editor
Michael L. Peterson
Asbury Theological Seminary

Michael L. Peterson is Professor of Philosophy at Asbury Theological Seminary. He is the author of *God and Evil* (Routledge); *Monotheism, Suffering, and Evil* (Cambridge University Press); *With All Your Mind* (University of Notre Dame Press); *C. S. Lewis and the Christian Worldview* (Oxford University Press); *Evil and the Christian God* (Baker Book House); and *Philosophy of Education: Issues and Options* (Intervarsity Press). He is co-author of *Reason and Religious Belief* (Oxford University Press); *Science, Evolution, and Religion: A Debate about Atheism and Theism* (Oxford University Press); and *Biology, Religion, and Philosophy* (Cambridge University Press). He is editor of *The Problem of Evil: Selected Readings* (University of Notre Dame Press). He is co-editor of *Philosophy of Religion: Selected Readings* (Oxford University Press) and *Contemporary Debates in Philosophy of Religion* (Wiley-Blackwell). He served as General Editor of the Blackwell monograph series Exploring Philosophy of Religion and is founding Managing Editor of the journal *Faith and Philosophy.*

About the Series
This series explores problems related to God, such as the human quest for God or gods, contemplation of God, and critique and rejection of God. Concise, authoritative volumes in this series will reflect the methods of a variety of disciplines, including philosophy of religion, theology, religious studies, and sociology.

Cambridge Elements ≡

The Problems of God

Elements in the Series

A full series listing is available at: www.cambridge.org/EPOG.

Printed in the United States
by Baker & Taylor Publisher Services